The Words and Music of Sting

The Words and Music of Sting

Christopher Gable

James E. Perone, Series Editor

Westport, Connecticut
London

Library of Congress Cataloging-in-Publication Data

Gable, Christopher, 1968–
    The words and music of Sting / Christopher Gable.
        p.   cm. — (The Praeger singer-songwriter collection, ISSN 1553–3484)
    Includes bibliographical references, discography, filmography, and index.
    ISBN 978–0–275–99360–3 (alk. paper)
    1. Sting (Musician)—Criticism and interpretation.   2. Rock music—
History and criticism   I. Title.
ML420.S847G33   2009
782.42166092—dc22   2008037530

British Library Cataloguing in Publication Data is available.

Library of Congress Catalog Card Number: 2008037530
ISBN: 978–0–275–99360–3
ISSN: 1553–3484

First published in 2009

Praeger Publishers, 88 Post Road West, Westport, CT 06881
An imprint of Greenwood Publishing Group, Inc.
www.praeger.com

Printed in the United States of America

The paper used in this book complies with the
Permanent Paper Standard issued by the National
Information Standards Organization (Z39.48–1984).

10   9   8   7   6   5   4   3   2   1

For my brother Ted, who first turned me on to The Police
and went with me to the *Synchronicity* concert at Hollywood Park.
He would have liked this.
And for Cora, who I hope will read this someday.

Contents

Series Foreword

Although the term, *Singer-Songwriters,* might most frequently be associated with a cadre of musicians of the early 1970s such as Paul Simon, James Taylor, Carly Simon, Joni Mitchell, Cat Stevens, and Carole King, the Praeger Singer-Songwriter Collection defines singer-songwriters more broadly, both in terms of style and in terms of time period. The series includes volumes on musicians who have been active from approximately the 1960s through the present. Musicians who write and record in folk, rock, soul, hip-hop, country, and various hybrids of these styles will be represented. Therefore, some of the early 1970s introspective singer-songwriters named above will be included, but not exclusively.

What do the individuals included in this series have in common? Some have never collaborated as writers. But, while some have done so, all have written and recorded commercially successful and/or historically important music *and* lyrics at some point in their careers.

The authors who contribute to the series also exhibit diversity. Some are scholars who are trained primarily as musicians, while others have such areas of specialization as American studies, history, sociology, popular culture studies, literature, and rhetoric. The authors share a high level of scholarship, accessibility in their writing, and a true insight into the work of the artists they study. The authors are also focused on the output of their subjects and how it relates to their subject's biography and the society around them; however, biography in and of itself is not a major focus of the books in this series.

Given the diversity of the musicians who are the subject of books in this series, and given the diversity of viewpoint of the authors, volumes in the

series will differ from book to book. All, however, will be organized chrono-
logically around the compositions and recorded performances of their subjects. All of the books in the series should also serve as listeners' guides to
the music of their subjects, making them companions to the artists' recorded
output.

James E. Perone
Series Editor

Acknowledgments

Writing a first book is possibly a bit like being plunked down on a sailboat on the open water and expected to bring the thing back to the dock. One has a general idea where to go and how to get there (by the wind), but one doesn't know which rope to pull or which way starboard is. I would like to thank the following deckhands, navigators, and able bodies for their invaluable help: Mark Mazullo, Phil Ford, Barb Peterson, Tricia Davis-Muffett and Carroll Muffett, Kat Jayne of Jayne Indexing, James Perone, my editor Dan Harmon, my students at Macalester, and many friends and colleagues who have offered encouragement and ideas. Long-term thanks also to Steven Schmidt, who many years ago encouraged me to stay in music, and who drove us to the *Synchronicity* concert.

Especially grateful thank yous go to my parents and "the in-laws" (who don't live up to the traditional connotations of the term). Jan and Dave Kirby and Dorothy Taylour have been constant sources of love, laughter, and inspiration throughout this voyage. My parents, Fred and Barbara Gable, have made the wind blow in the right direction to get the ship going again with their financial support, encouragement, and guidance. Thanks for those viola lessons that got me started on this musical journey!

And the person who has been on deck the most, without whom this ship would be stranded at sea, is my wife Merie Kirby. Muse, guide, Mommy, sounding board, typist, lifeblood, bibliographic assistant, editor, soul mate. This book is really a collaboration between us, in the truest sense of the word.

Introduction

It's very hard to talk about music in words. Words are superfluous to the abstract power of music. We can fashion words into poetry so that they are understood the way music is understood, but they only aspire to the condition where music already exists.[1]

> —Sting, "The Mystery and Religion of Music"
> (Berklee College of Music commencement address,
> May 15, 1994)

What is music? It's a journey.[2]

> —Sting, *The Journey & the Labyrinth:*
> *The Music of John Dowland*

In late 2006, many Sting fans were perhaps surprised that his new album was a recording of Renaissance lute songs by John Dowland. Here was an international superstar, a veteran of the music and film industries, an environmental and human rights activist and award-winning songwriter with a practically guaranteed fan base, sitting down with a Bosnian lutenist to sing 400-year-old love songs. But, after the initial surprise, those who were familiar with Sting's career trajectory could undoubtedly see the logic behind his new choice of repertoire. For he has always been a risk-taker, both professionally and artistically. His restless energy has served him well and forced him on to hitherto unforeseen paths. He has described himself as a lifelong learner,[3] and this curiosity has not let him stagnate for lack of creative direction. Sting's interest in John Dowland (1563–1626) will be explored further in the conclusion to this book. For now the pertinent element of this project is Sting's identification with Dowland as a fellow singer-songwriter.

The singer-songwriter tradition as we commonly know it began in the 1960s, with the folk revival. It is often associated with a simple instrumentation of a singer accompanying themselves with a guitar, and Woody Guthrie seems to be the grandfather of the genre. Like a Wagner opera on a much smaller scale, these songs are their own *Gesamtkunstwerk,* where every note, word, and performance is by the singer-songwriter. From Guthrie and Pete Seeger's influence grew seminal figures of the 1960s like Bob Dylan, Joan Baez, and Paul Simon. The instrumentation eventually expanded to include other accompanying instruments besides guitar, and some singer-songwriters recorded and performed with a backup band. Still, no matter how complex the arrangements became, the crucial element of the genre is that the singer wrote both words and music. In a typical "group" situation it is more of a collective effort, with more collaboration on the writing of songs and different songwriting credits from song to song.

This distinction is important, because a large part of the singer-songwriter's aesthetic is that of personal expression. In the 1970s, with artists like Joni Mitchell and James Taylor leading the way, the "confessional" mode became the order of the day. Intensely personal, sometimes political subject matter was delivered in the most intimate of ways—directly to the listener's speakers or headphones.

The reader may be a bit surprised to find Sting included in this series on the singer-songwriter. After all, he initially became famous as a member of The Police, one of the most successful groups in popular music history. But he was, like Paul Simon, the primary songwriter for the larger outfit, and he ultimately gave in to his urge to become a solo artist. He has been described as the child that Joni Mitchell and James Taylor never had.[4]

The music, words, and life of many singer-songwriters are inextricably linked. Sting is no exception. Many of his confessional songs have connections to events in his personal life; these connections are either explicit or implicit. This book will serve as a kind of "road map" through Sting's life-journey thus far—the signposts being his primary mode of expression: his songs. As we all know, people change over the course of their lives—we develop new interests and new friends, and these new experiences become part of us. Yet despite changes over a person's lifetime, people also, paradoxically, remain the same. In the following pages we will discover how Sting's music and choice of subject matter change: from reggae to jazz to country, from lyrics focused on the self to songs about universal love. At the same time, I believe it is possible to discern a through-line in the songs of Sting—examples where similar lyric content occurs over the course of many years, as well as songs that refer musically back to a previous chord progression, melody, riff, or general mood.

This book is not a biography per se; that task has been adequately completed by many other previous writers, including Sting himself, in his memoir *Broken Music* (2003). However, it includes biographical information as it pertains to Sting's creative output. I focus on his career as a solo artist, but also discuss (later in this introduction) his beginnings as a struggling jazz musician and school teacher in the Newcastle region and his subsequent move to London and joining The Police. It must not go unsaid that he would not be where he is today without his seven-plus years as a member of The Police; however, his ambition to become a solo artist was constantly with him and was a major factor in the breakup of the group.

As Sting suggests in the first epigraph above, music is difficult to write about. Despite being performed on very concrete instruments, music itself is an abstract art. In writing about music, writers try to capture at least a portion of not only the meanings of notes and words, but also the emotions evoked and the very essence of the art form. Throughout this book, I am assuming a familiarity with the songs that I discuss and that the reader will have ready access to recordings of The Police and Sting. Because of this, and because of the focus of this series on singer-songwriters, I have concentrated on only the most important Police tracks and on almost all of Sting's solo songs that are readily available. B-sides and miscellaneous soundtrack songs are thus given much less attention. I will essentially provide the reader with a listening guide to Sting's primary body of work. I feel that a chronological approach best reflects his growth as a songwriter: from the punk/reggae hybrid of early Police songs, to his embrace of musical "Britishism" in his middle solo career, to his use of non-Western music, and to his eventual arrival on the stage of adult contemporary rock.

After a brief biographical sketch at the end of this introduction, chapter 1 will examine Sting's major contributions to The Police, up through *Ghost in the Machine* (1981). Chapter 2 focuses on a few representative songs from the height of The Police's fame and their strongest and final album, *Synchronicity* (1983). Chapters 3 and 4 discuss his entry into the world of the "solo artist" with his first three studio albums as well as the live album *Bring on the Night* (1986). Chapter 5, after the darkness of *The Soul Cages* (1991), sees a new life and success for Sting in the 1990s. The final chapter, chapter 6, deals with his most recent two solo albums and their varying degrees of success. In the conclusion, I use the Dowland exploration as an example of his never-satisfied search for creative knowledge.

One of my main goals in teaching my undergraduate music theory classes has been to help the students to understand *why* they like a piece of music. Rather than simply expressing an opinion, I want them to be able to explain how a song or piece of classical music works. They should be able to articulate, as specifically as possible, what makes a song special, unique, or representative of its composer and the era from which it came. I have tried to do this in the following pages. Sting's music has been with us for a sufficient amount of time now for us as listeners to move beyond simply "I like that song" to a more fundamental understanding of his musical and textual expression.

Since I am a music theorist and composer by training, I will approach each song through the lens of music theory. While that includes discussions of chord progressions, key areas, large-scale formal structure, uses of scales and modes, and rhythmic patterns, these discussions are geared toward the layperson. Western popular music, by its very nature and in the way that most of it is composed, is primarily harmony (chord) based. The vast majority of songs are written and worked out on a guitar. This instrument, in earlier folk and country music from which rock 'n' roll derived, is largely strummed. Thus the bedrock of a popular song is a sequence of strummed chords: its harmonic structure. In this study, then, melody occupies a slightly less important slot in the analyses. Throughout I will use the standard practice of labeling major chords with capital letters and minor chords with lowercase letters.

In order not to be too technical, I will eschew the use of notated musical examples and will define the more obscure musical terms not readily known by the layperson. I have found in my experience that technical music jargon is often used for fairly simple concepts. It is my belief that with a little explanation and a good set of ears, most listeners can grasp a fairly complex song with a concentrated effort. Sting is certainly an artist whose work stands up to this type of attention. Those readers who still feel some confusion in spite of my definitions may wish to simply skim or skip those paragraphs that seem too technical. After all, the ultimate goal of this book is a deeper appreciation of Sting's songwriting and artistry. His songs, like many of his forbears in the singer-songwriter tradition (Joni Mitchell, James Taylor, Paul Simon), work great as radio-friendly pop but also reward deeper analysis. It is not just any songwriter who can seamlessly combine Jungian archetypes with allusions to Shakespeare, Homer, the Faust legend, the Bible, and T. S. Eliot in a catchy song. And those are just the textual references. Musically, he draws on an array of stylistic traditions, sometimes multiple styles in one song. In his best songs, all of these musical and stylistic choices are in service to the text: getting the message across in the immediate medium of popular song.

One of my main goals for this book is to point out Sting's use of metaphor in his songs. It is one of his favorite rhetorical tropes and is an essential tool in every writer's tool bag. He uses it to engage his listeners; to make them think about what they are hearing. My contention is that Sting uses metaphor not only in a traditional poetic sense but also in a musical way. Now, I am not claiming that he is the first to do so. The Beatles were masters at this type of layered meaning that they elicited from a song's text, through harmony, melody, texture, and rhythm. My model in this regard is the musicologist Walter Everett, who with his two-volume study of The Beatles "as composers" set the gold standard for in-depth deconstruction of the popular song.[5] Metaphor in music is all over the place for Everett.

My approach, unlike Everett's, is geared toward the lay-listener and avid fan of Sting and The Police. I hope that I use just enough musical language to make the essential point of each song, and that those songs that use music metaphorically will be able to be grasped with a minimum of musical training. After all, the main point of this book is interpretation, along with appreciation. My interpretation is only one of many, but since Sting's songs have not been studied so closely up to now, I feel that this is a worthwhile contribution to the field.

Alongside Sting's career as a musician, and in many ways complementary to it, is his legacy as a visual icon. Popular music is of course not just about the sounds coming out of the speakers. The concept of the image, both literal and figurative, in pop music dates back at least to Elvis Presley's hips and pouting lower lip. The use of Sting's image to promote his music (and that of The Police prior to his solo career) is part of a proven track record of the music industry selling an image as well as the record. The success of this can be attested to by Sting's crossover career in films.[6] A true structuralist study of Sting's iconic power is beyond the scope of this book, but it warrants mention as making up the identity of the person and the artist.

Rather than try to outdo Sting himself in providing a biography, I will not recount in detail his childhood and upbringing in the 1950s and 60s in the Newcastle area in the north of England. I refer the reader who wants to learn more to Sting's memoir, *Broken Music*. It is an excellent book; a study of a complex man and where he came from. Honest and revealing, it traces his early life from working for his father, the dairyman, all the way up to his eventual encounter with Stewart Copeland and the formation of The Police. And it does so with remarkable candor, which is a rarity among rock star autobiographies.

Suffice it to say that Gordon Matthew Sumner was born in October of 1951 to working-class parents in the midst of shipyards, factories, and dairyman routes. His was not a privileged upbringing. In fact, he seems to have worked nearly every day of his life. Introduced to the piano through his mother, he eventually acquired a guitar from a family friend and obsessively played it when he should have been studying. He attended grammar school and college in Newcastle—all the while playing music with anyone else he could. The choice of bass as an instrument was by chance,[7] but it has served him well over the years. Most young popular musicians with stars in their eyes take up the guitar (which he also plays), but Sting probably found more gigs and got more experience by sticking with the more reserved and less flashy bass. He was given his stage name by another Gordon, Gordon Solomon, the leader of the Phoenix Jazzmen. Sting's favorite yellow-and-brown striped sweater apparently reminded the bandleader of a wasp. While attending a teacher's college for three years, he met his main musical colleague and early collaborator, Gerry Richardson.[8] It is with this keyboard player and songwriter that he eventually formed the jazz-rock band Last Exit. They achieved a small amount of success, although mostly concentrated in regional venues. Gradually, Sting began singing more often during their sets, and eventually he was known officially as the lead singer. So Sting's primary musical experience prior to The Police was in neither punk nor reggae; rather he was well-versed in jazz, soul, and fusion.

His marriage in 1976 to actress Frances Tomelty (whom he met while playing in the pit orchestra for a musical) proved to be fortuitous to his future career. It was she who urged the young couple to move to London to further her acting interests (in January 1977)[9] and actually inspired Sting to later follow suit. Stewart Copeland, in Newcastle for a show with his band Curved Air, was impressed enough with Sting's performance that he told him to look him up if he ever got down to London. The rest is history, as they say. This chance meeting seems almost as significant as John Lennon and Paul McCartney's first meeting at a Liverpool church social in 1957. Sting's move to London was a momentous decision, and it involved him giving up the relative security of his teaching job at a parochial school and jumping head first into the London music scene. Last Exit tried to stay together and had some successful gigs, but it was only a few months before the glamorous bass player with the nicely developing tenor voice would part ways with his friend and mentor, Gerry Richardson.

The Police, as Copeland had always wanted to call his band, originally included a guitarist, Henry Padovani; a good-looking "Corsican pirate" (Sting's words).[10] Unfortunately, he apparently was not as talented as he was attractive. Copeland's oldest brother Miles was already an established producer and manager by the time Sting met him. Miles Copeland played as big or bigger a role in Sting's later career as did Stewart. He became Sting's manager for the majority of his solo years. Stewart and Sting met Andy Summers through Sting's publisher, Carol Wilson.[11] At first they tried to use both Summers and Padovani, but after a chaotic tour of France as a support act in the summer of 1977, it soon became clear that Padovani was dead weight.[12] Besides, Copeland's original idea for the band was a trio. He was attracted to the challenge and simplicity of the format, inspired by legendary "power trios" of the past: The Jimi Hendrix Experience and Cream. Copeland was eager to create a three-piece band that would channel the energy of punk but would create a new sound.

Along with Sting's memoir, Summers has contributed his own autobiography, *One Train Later.* This 2006 book goes into much more detail of The Police years, with numerous scenes of rock star excess and especially fascinating descriptions of the contentious recording sessions of the group's final two albums: "In truth, we are like children locked in a house with big shiny machines and a handful of explosives."[13] It is an often painful account of a musician's life that seems choked by fame. But it also presents a catalog of signs and hints along the way of Sting's uneasiness with being "in a band."

But what a band it was. Like Sting, both Summers and Copeland came from areas very different from punk or reggae. Copeland was the drummer of the art-rock band Curved Air, and Summers had had years of experience playing all sorts of music, from psychedelic rock and jazz to early New Age (Mike Oldfield's *Tubular Bells*) and blues-rock (as a member of Eric Burdon and The Animals). This wealth of experience from all three members of The Police contributed to their unique sound. In 1977, when they first met, punk was a relatively new phenomenon. Its credo was to destroy everything that happened before, ostensibly to create something new. Musicality and actually knowing how to play were considered liabilities in the punk ethos. At the same time, Jamaican immigrants were making inroads into the London music scene, playing this very different style of music called reggae. Bob Marley was becoming a major international star.

So the three-piece lineup was set, the first couple of singles were on the radio, and they eventually clicked as a trio, with Sting's songwriting flowering under the newfound simplicity of the instrumentation. It was only a matter of time before Sting and his bandmates had created enough material (some of which was based on Sting's earlier Last Exit songs) to fill an album. They scraped up enough money to record it at a small studio in the suburbs of London and did it at night to get a cheaper rate. Miles Copeland had reluctantly agreed to release the singles on his label, Illegal Records; but he was reluctant only until he heard one of the new tracks: "Roxanne." With that song, he knew they had a hit, and he promptly got them signed to A&M Records.

The Police

The seeds of everything Sting has written as a solo artist are to be found in his songs on the five albums and B-sides by The Police. Everything from an identification with the working class to the recurrent theme of loneliness is part of that group of songs. In general, the Police songs get increasingly complex in structure, although there are always exceptions on each album. Also, the more refined production values and generally "softer" sound of *Synchronicity* seem to come from a very different band than the raw, quasi-punk aesthetic of *Outlandos d'Amour*. This is not surprising, given the shoestring budget of the first album as well as *Synchronicity*'s use of digital technology (in both the synthesizers and recording equipment).

In this chapter I will focus on several significant Sting compositions from his Police period; a few "focus songs" from each album. By significant I mean either musically or textually important in light of his future output. I will make connections between otherwise disparate songs.

Much has been written regarding The Police's incorporation of reggae into their early songs. Some writers like to describe them as a "reggae-punk hybrid."[1] The truth is that the band merely utilized the trappings of 1970s British punk: the bleached-blond short hair, Sting in his jumpsuits or army jackets, Copeland and his near maniacal drumming style. In fact, they were criticized by other punk bands for not being authentic and for lacking "street cred."[2] The majority of their musical influences can be traced to Bob Marley, The Beatles, pub rock, jazz, and a hint of progressive rock. The punk aesthetic, with its call for anarchy, revolution, destruction, and noise, is fairly far away from the sensibilities of a song like "Hole in My Life." The punk element was primarily present in the "look" of the band (which includes the rough-hewn quality of their first album cover and lyric sleeve).

The three men were much more conscious of incorporating the relatively recent style of reggae into their music. As Copeland said in 1981, "Most music is a hybrid of one kind or another. It's when you choose ingredients that are less used-up that you get more interesting results."[3] What The Police did perhaps take from punk was a certain brand of nervous, energetic disillusion with 1970s Britain. Many songs (almost all from *Outlandos*) were up-tempo, despite such heavy subject matter as emptiness, unrequited love, suicide (although rhetorical), drugs, and prostitution.

OUTLANDOS D'AMOUR

Throughout this book I will discuss the rhetorical device of the non-trustworthy narrator and the idea of narrative "voice" in a lyric, which is rarely the same as a singer of a given song. On The Police's first album, *Outlandos d'Amour*, several songs use this technique. For example, Sting never actually knew a prostitute named "Roxanne," but he used the voice of a man who is in love with her to construct a song that tells a story as old as love itself. The theme of forbidden love is quite common in Sting's work, and "Roxanne" is the earliest and probably the most famous example.

An element of the song that deepens its richness is the implication that, even though Roxanne and the speaker are in a romantic relationship, she apparently has been a prostitute for some time. One assumes that the couple met first during a paid sexual encounter; at least that is how this story usually goes. So the implication is that the speaker has finally come to an emotional place where he cannot stand it any longer, that he must say what he thinks before it's too late. The speaker feels trapped by an untenable situation, and the only way to break through to Roxanne is to use song to express himself. In this respect, "Roxanne" resembles an opera aria or musical theater song, in which the character simply has no other recourse to affect or change a situation but to sing.

Musically, the song relates to and illustrates the text in subtle and remarkable ways. The verses cycle through a descending eight-bar pattern of bass notes (taken from the g-minor scale), only to end up each time back where it started, on the initial g. The speaker states the bleak situation of his emotions (in the present), but those emotions are incapable of changing the outcome (represented by being harmonically "stuck" in the key of g minor). The chorus, on the other hand, speaks about the future and the hope that Roxanne will change her lifestyle and leave the streets. The speaker is imploring (repeatedly) the woman to see that she has choices: She doesn't "have to put on the red light." The "red light" in this song represents prostitution as an occupation. It is legal in most European countries, and most cities have specifically designated areas of town where it is allowed, indicated by actual red light bulbs in the women's "storefronts." These women are given routine physicals and medical testing to prevent the spread of disease and drug abuse. Other areas of town of course contain undocumented prostitution. Thus, if we interpret the red light literally, Roxanne is a legal prostitute.

Moreover, the chorus is, stylistically, completely contrasting with the reggae-derived verses. The choruses refer to a hard-driving rock idiom sometimes referred to as "pub rock," popular among British bar bands in the late 1970s (although not necessarily commercially successful). It was akin to punk in many ways (in fact, punk probably derived from it) but lacked the nihilism and general tendency toward revolution that punk aspired to. In any case, the operative word here is "contrast." The speaker uses this completely different style of music to express his feelings about the future; namely, the hope for a better life away from the world of prostitution, and by extension a life with him, the speaker.

The irony of this chorus, however, is that it is, as the verses are, "stuck" in a harmonic cycle (of B♭, F, and g minor), never deviating from this sequence of chords and never settling on a "home" key. In a traditional, classical harmonic context, a song in a minor key would have a major key that could provide a possible "escape" from the dark colors of the home key. (Indeed, as we shall see, in his best songs, Sting borrows heavily from this "classical" tradition of harmony to construct meaning.) This major key is considered closely related to the minor one because it shares a key signature with it (and therefore generally uses the same seven pitches in its scale). The term for this relationship between keys (and between scales) is "relative." In the case of "Roxanne," the home key is g minor (key signature of two flats), and the relative major key to this is B♭. The chorus's progression of B♭ F g thus hints at a possible shift to the key of B♭, especially with its statement of an F chord, which is a chord built on the fifth scale degree (B♭ C D E♭ F) of B♭. This chord (the "five" chord), in any key, has a special place in the relative importance of chords. It is, after the tonic (the "home" chord), the next most important harmony within a given key.

A fascinating aspect of this chorus is that it ends the song during the fade-out. The fade-out itself is not an especially unique feature. Countless popular songs since the late 1950s utilized the fade-out as a way to end a song. It offered radio disc jockeys an efficient way to segue between songs without any dead air space. But in the reading of the chorus/verse relationship outlined above, the fade-out implies that the speaker is continuing his search for that better life but is unable to attain it (at least in the context of this song).

Another equally interesting element of this chorus fade-out is its conflicting levels of large-scale rhythmic grouping. Many songs, including this one, use a pattern of four-bar units (or four groups of four beats each). "Roxanne" uses this pattern for the entire first part of the song, in both the verses and chorus:

Verse:	bar:	1	2	3	4	5	6	7	8				
	bass:	G	F	E♭	D	C	F	G	G				
Chorus:	bar:	1	2	3	4	5	6	7	8	1	2	3	4
	bass:	B♭		F		G		B♭		F		G	

In both cases, g is the goal. The difference in the fade-out chorus is that the chord pattern never "ends"—it just repeats and fades out, implying continuation. Since there are only three chords in the pattern, however, there is a rhythmic conflict of three against four (or more accurately, six bars against eight):

Fade-out Chorus

bar:	1	2	3	4	5	6	7	8
bass:	B♭		F		G		B♭	
bar:	9	10	11	12	1	2	3	4	5 . . .
bass:	F		G		B♭		F		G . . .

Here, there is no goal as such, both harmonically and in the large-scale rhythmic grouping. This is another example of the speaker's inability to break out of the situation, being constrained by both the key of g minor (never confidently attaining the "release" of B♭ major) and the pervasive pattern of four or eight bar groupings forever in conflict with the three-chord sequence of the fade-out chorus. So the search for a better life continues and in fact could be less secure (implied by the harmonic instability) than the present state of affairs.

Outlandos d'Amour contains several other songs that, like "Roxanne," include a reggae influence. Songs that display this reggae style include: "So Lonely" (similar in structure to "Roxanne," with reggae verses and a rock chorus), "Can't Stand Losing You," and "Hole in My Life."

This last song is a good example of Sting's predilection for up-tempo songs with rather sad lyrics. The words speak of loneliness and unattainable love, and loneliness (and perhaps lust) is compared to having a disease. The implication is that the "hole" the speaker sings of can be filled by an unspoken "you" (the object of his desire).

As mentioned above, the bouncy, faux-reggae rhythm, typified by Copeland's cymbal/snare hits on beat four, plays against the professed loneliness of the protagonist. Indeed, Sting's repeated "yeahs" are about as positive and ecstatic as one can get. And they seem to be related to the thought of the "hole" being in the guy's life. However, these outbursts could also be interpreted as "Yeah! You're the one!"

Summers's guitar features prominently throughout the song, and one cannot help but wonder if he had a hand in its composition and guitar voicing, albeit uncredited. At the very opening one can hear the "flanging" effect on the guitar quite clearly. The flange is a standard effects-box gadget that modifies one's guitar sound before it gets to the amplifier. In this case, the flange-box immediately replicates the sound, like an incredibly fast echo. The unit can be adjusted to produce a resultant sound that slowly changes the "EQ" (or equalization) of the sound so that lower and then higher frequencies are alternately emphasized.[4] Constantly changing the "treble" and "bass" dials on a stereo amplifier gives a similar effect. These opening two alternating chords pretty much define the song. Added to this a couple bars later are Sting's signature sparse yet melodic bass riff and Copeland's reggae-inspired drum pattern, full of inventive subdivisions of the beat and the ever-present crashes on beat four.

The "middle" section (sometimes known as the "bridge"), which starts with the words "There's something missing in my life" is the most interesting section harmonically. The essential chords of this section are D and E, which alternate four times. However, Sting's bass note on the first two chords of each group of four articulate the fifth of each chord, not the root as is normally the case in rock music. This subtle change coincides with the textural change of this "middle." The guitar becomes more broadly stroked, and the cymbal crashes become, if possible, even more pronounced. This leads back into the chorus material, with its pattern based on D, and the long-held vocal notes over a descending bass line.

Some notable features of the ending of "Hole in My Life" are its gradual slowdown in the last eight bars and the multi-tracked "cluster" chord of Sting's voice, which presents every note of the scale that the song is based on (a, g, f♯, e, d, c, b = a Dorian). This type of ending is reminiscent of Paul McCartney's similarly multi-tracked voice at the end of "Love You To," a George Harrison song from the album *Revolver.* The multi-tracked vocal technique of "Hole in My Life" generally prefigures many of the songs on later Police albums, especially *Ghost in the Machine.* Sting's interest in this form of "choral" singing has continued all the way up to 2006 with his multi-tracked rendition of John Dowland's "Can She Excuse My Wrongs?"

My only criticism of "Hole in My Life" is that the contrasting middle section, while musically interesting, does not include a new train of thought in the speaker's mind. He is still talking about the "hole," although using different words to describe it. In the tradition of Broadway and Tin Pan Alley songs, a change in texture goes hand in hand with a change in thought, mood, or subject matter. In later years (and certainly with the above example of "Roxanne"), Sting has been much more aware of this technique and has used it quite effectively in several of his solo songs.

Reggatta de Blanc

The Police's second album, *Reggatta de Blanc,* was released in October 1979, exactly a year after their debut. Once again it was recorded at Surrey Sound with the help of Nigel Gray; again it had a quasi-multilingual title (this time implying "white reggae"); and again the cover art featured the three band members' close-up headshots. Also similar to the first album is its alternation of hard-driving rock with reggae-inspired numbers. In fact the reggae influence seems more prominent here, appearing on 5 of the 11 tracks. However, this collection feels less focused and in general seems to be simply a showcase for the two strongest songs on the album, which were also the first two singles. I mean, of course, "Message in a Bottle," their first UK No. 1, and "Walking on the Moon." Many of the other songs feel like filler but include compositions by Copeland and Summers.

"Message in a Bottle" is, like "Eleanor Rigby" of the previous decade, one of the great songs in the popular tradition that deal with loneliness. On the surface, the song is told from the perspective of a castaway on a desert island. He talks about his loneliness, but soon it's apparent that he is talking to a lover (or potential lover), wanting to be rescued from a metaphorical island. Still, even though the rhetorical device is acknowledged by the speaker, he continues to use it to make his point. Similarly to "Roxanne," the chorus is used as a harbinger of hope that the situation will be improved (in the former case, by escape; in this case, by rescue). At the end of the chorus the speaker mentions for the first time the title of the song, at the same time that the harmony "slips" or "deflates" back to the home key of c♯ minor. It should also be mentioned that the appearance of the words "Message in a Bottle" happens after a couple of repeated and increasingly insistent fragments: "I'll send an S.O.S. to the world" and "I hope that someone gets my . . ." The second verse seems more generalized, focusing on the nature of love in the abstract.

Before the final verse (and after the second chorus), Summers plays an extra bar of an f♯ minor chord, which serves to quiet the mood a bit before the crucial point of the song. The speaker finds, after waking up "this morning" (giving a temporal context to the song), millions of bottles (one assumes with messages in them) from lonely people just like himself. Again the conceit of "Eleanor Rigby" can be recalled, in that there are lonely people everywhere, all "looking for a home" as Sting sings. The irony is that millions of people feel "alone"—a typical sentiment and effect of modern life in the Western world. The song does not pretend to offer a solution, just an observation. The implied solution is that of love: what the speaker sought in the beginning. Love can break down barriers between people and hopefully lead to a less lonely world. This song is a great example of Sting's ability to take the ethos of a popular love song (as it seems to be in the beginning) and expand it to encompass the whole world in a statement of universal compassion.

Musically, "Message in a Bottle" revolves around its opening—and extremely difficult—guitar riff. Occasionally, Summers uses a guitar synthesizer that creates a kind of "copy" of the riff, a fifth above the original. In the popular musician's terminology, this riff would be described as "busy"—a general term that essentially means several different notes inside of the beat.

This "busy-ness" of the music plays against the metaphorical setting of the deserted island. Copeland's "double-time" style of drumming (on this song especially) propels the band forward with his constant quarter-note bass drum strokes. The busy sound of the music perhaps refers not to the deserted island, but to modern urban life and all the lonely souls on their own separate islands.

As mentioned above, the chorus implies a hope of rescue from this loneliness. As in "Roxanne," the reggae-style beat is smoothly transformed into a straight-ahead rock groove. "Message in a Bottle" also begins the chorus in the relative major key of A. But it ends back in c♯ minor, coinciding with the title of the song (as stated earlier), as well as a switch back to the reggae beat. Another difference here is that this song ends with the opening guitar riff as opposed to a fade-out of the chorus, as in "Roxanne." Also, Sting repeats the phrase "sending out an S.O.S.," implying that the speaker's situation has not changed. Mournful, plaintive guitar work floats high above the mix through the latter half of the song, poignantly illustrating the thoughts of the speaker.

Loneliness is an undercurrent in *Reggatta de Blanc*'s other major UK hit single, "Walking on the Moon." Although a relationship is central to this song, the speaker again feels alone, as if living on the moon. The difference here is that the man is stating the desire to be "alone" with his lover on the moon. This is in general a much less serious song than "Message." The whimsical element is evident in the third line: "I hope my legs don't break" from the "giant steps" in the low gravity of the moon. Realistically, one would more likely be concerned with oxygen supply, whether the capsule has enough fuel to get back home to Earth, and other mundane topics such as those. But, as Sting sings in the chorus, "I may as well play."

This chorus, incidentally, is another one that uses the relative major to the home key (here, d minor). This harmonic shift (to B♭) provides a welcome contrast to the alternating d minor and C chords of the introduction and verses (although Summers's guitar elegantly alternates between sustained chords and short, rhythmic ones). It also coincides with a lyrical shift in focus: The chorus is centered around what other people's criticisms might be if the speaker moved with his lover to the moon. The cycle of chords ends with the line "I may as well play" on a C chord, which transitions easily back into the verse material and the associated long chords from Summers. It is Summers who, I feel, really sets the atmosphere of this song. Copeland lays down an intricate and fascinating reggae beat, which subtly changes throughout the song. Add to that Sting's soaring melody and enigmatic "keep it up" of the coda, and we have one of The Police's compellingly mysterious songs.

The verses deserve more mention. Sting treats the refrain/title in both a literal and metaphorical way. The first verse, as mentioned, deals with the actual effects of low gravity on humans while on the lunar surface. Sting was more than likely remembering footage from the moonwalks during the Apollo missions between 1969 and 1972. The bouncing, almost floating nature of these missions is used metaphorically in the second verse. This woman makes the speaker feel as if he's bouncing home in low gravity. This is what inspires him to want to live there with her, away from all distractions.

Sting changes the melody each time the refrain of "Walking on the Moon" returns, which provides musical interest as well as accentuating the differences in sentence construction. In the first verse the word "walking" is actually part of each sentence; in the first two lines of the second verse, "walking" is more of a fragmented simile: "Walking back from your house [is like] walking on the moon."

ZENYATTA MONDATTA

In early 1980, The Police embarked on a world tour, the scope and scale of which rivaled some of the later Beatles tours. In March 1980 they became the first Western band to play in Bombay (Mumbai), India. Due in part to Miles Copeland's connections with foreign diplomats (through the Copelands' father), they played in countries not normally on the typical pop band's itinerary at the time. This tour included stops in Cairo, Hong Kong, Tokyo, Athens, Mexico, New Zealand, and Australia. Sting's and Miles Copeland's predilection for performing in "out of the way" places continued into the twenty-first century. Sting's *Sacred Love* tour of 2003–2005 traveled to places as unusual (for a concert tour, anyway) as Lithuania, Romania, Portugal, and Morocco.

During the 1980 tour, The Police managed to sneak in some studio time in Holland to record their third album, *Zenyatta Mondatta*. This time, the nonsensical album title is a hybrid of the words Zen, Kenyatta (from the name of the former dictator of Kenya, Jomo Kenyatta), and *monde* (French for "world"). It playfully refers to the group's seemingly unquenchable wanderlust.

This album is similar to *Reggatta de Blanc* in many ways: two big singles, a couple of other decent songs, but the rest filler. Some of it is very good filler, but not musically or lyrically very interesting. However, the success of the two singles "De Do Do Do, De Da Da Da" (No. 10 on the Billboard chart) and "Don't Stand So Close To Me" (also No. 10) propelled this album to the band's highest chart position thus far, peaking at No. 5 on the Billboard album chart.[5]

The first single from the new album, "De Do Do Do, De Da Da Da," makes an interesting comparison to earlier reggae/rock hybrids such as "Roxanne" or "So Lonely." These earlier songs featured reggae-inspired verses with pub rock choruses. "De Do Do Do" uses the same musical contrast technique, but this time the chorus is pure pop confection. "Harmless" and "meaningless" are words that come to mind, and "their innocence" and meaninglessness are explicitly stated in the lyrics of the chorus. However, I think Sting is saying something more significant about words and language. As Sting writes in his introduction to the song in *Lyrics by Sting:* "I was trying to write an articulate song about being inarticulate."[6]

The words of the verse refer to madness ("banks of chaos in my mind"), authority figures (which have "words to thank for their positions"), and the power of language over people, which is likened to forcible rape. The chorus, on the other hand, states the speaker's true purpose of this song: innocence and meaninglessness. The implication is that sometimes we let language get in the way of our thoughts and the expression of our true feelings. It is not clear in this song what those feelings and thoughts actually are, but in the context of Sting's body of work, it is most likely about love. The contrast between the gravity of the verses' language and that of the chorus is perfectly expressed musically. The reggae beat and syncopated dissonance of Summers's guitar along with the implied key change to the relative minor of f♯ all provide a "misterioso" atmosphere that expresses this.

The innocence and catchiness of this song must have resonated with audiences, since it was The Police's first top-10 single in the United States. In this respect its precursors are the countless nonsense and patter songs of the 1950s and 60s early rock 'n' roll and pop charts, such as "De Do Run Run" and "Doo Wah Diddy." Sometimes fans don't want to think; they just want to sing along.

Before leaving the discussion of "De Do Do Do," the ending should be noted. The song ends with a fade-out of the "misterioso" verse mood and not the confectionery pop of the chorus. This is a remarkable feature that serves to undercut the frivolity and levity of the chorus. It also balances out the formal layout of the song. We started with the chorus music (functioning as the wordless introduction), and we end with the verse music as a wordless coda. Except for a short bridge section between the final two choruses, the amount of time spent on these two competing moods (and musical styles) is approximately equal. The minor key, "misterioso" ending also implies the continuing presence and our dependence on language. As this song shows, the only way to talk about language is to use it.

"Don't Stand So Close to Me" was the other successful single from *Zenyatta Mondatta.* Its subject is not a typical one for top-40 radio: a schoolgirl's obsession with a teacher. The omniscient observer of the lyric switches rapidly from the girl to the teacher, showing both sides of this sexual conflict. The three verses can generally be described, after an initial expository verse, as illustrating each of the character's social milieu and the problems that this infatuation engenders. So, the girl's friends are described as "jealous," and the teacher's colleagues are accusatory and the mood is tense. Sting provides a deft double entendre in the line: "You know how bad girls get." This phrase can refer both to a stereotype about "bad girls," or to the situation of jealousy and retribution that the girl finds herself in, making this reading mean "this is how mean-spirited girls can get in situations like this." The clipped, oblique nature of the lyric is best represented in the latter half of the second verse, where in opposition to the rain-sodden bus stop where the girl is waiting, "his car is warm and dry." The teacher's temptation is made almost palpable in these few words. The last line of the last verse refers to a "book by Nabokov," which of course is *Lolita*, the 1955 novel by Vladimir Nabokov (1899–1977) in which the main character, Humbert Humbert, harbors an infatuation with a young girl and then foolishly acts on it.

"Don't Stand So Close to Me" connects yet again with the recurrent theme of forbidden love in Sting's work. As in "Roxanne," the people (or characters) in the song are forbidden by social mores from pursuing or consummating their passion. Despite what the heart or the emotions tell them, external forces of social institutions (prostitution and teacher-student ethics) prevent the lovers from achieving happiness. The song also expresses the theme of temptation, which we will see is prominent in later Sting songs.

On the musical side, the verses carry most of the weight. This makes sense, since the chorus really only expresses one thought, and it does so in a very bouncy, pop style. Once again The Police are expressing rather gloomy sentiments with an infectious energy. The song includes a "mysterious" introduction that contains the prominent falling guitar motive, played arhythmically by Summers.[7] Although the sound quality of this album is generally higher than *Reggatta de Blanc*, this introduction displays some fairly sloppy recording and editing. At time point 0:22 one can hear a mistake in the low synthesizer note, briefly hitting a "g" instead of the $E\flat$. Whether this is due to bad editing or to a mistake in the performance is unclear. Also, there is a "ghostly" (i.e., very soft) drum set fragment that I am not sure was intended. Problems of this nature are generally solved in the mixing room, well after all the tracks have been recorded. Occasionally, however, mistakes do happen and find their way into the final mix. Even a normally meticulous band such as The Beatles has been known to release mixing mistakes. The album version of "Got to Get You into My Life" is a good example of this, where a very low-volume rhythm guitar part is audible throughout the song.[8]

Once Copeland's reggae beat begins, however, the song really takes off. The "mystery" of the alternating synth notes of $E\flat$ and G is answered by devoting two bars to each pitch. The falling guitar motive becomes the main verse melody. The melody pitches obstinately do not change with each bass note, even if they are dissonant with the bass. This I think represents the "circular" aspect of the situation. Everything the people in the song do can't seem to keep them away from each other, and thus they constantly become tempted.

In the chorus, the falling guitar and verse melody is transformed into a new key of D major, which implies a sort of escape from the "circle." But the stuttering, additive expression of the song's title in the chorus implies that the speaker(s) (indeed, the speaker of the title sentiment could be either the student or the teacher, though more likely the teacher) is at best unsure about his or her convictions. In the final chorus/fade-out, Sting sings a slower-moving countermelody above the chorus that we have heard previously. In classical music, this tune could be called a descant, which means a high-register countermelody normally sung by the soprano voices in a church choir setting during the last verse of a hymn. Sting's countermelody also vaguely reminds me of the technique of augmentation in which the main melody of a piece is played twice as slow (or even four times as slow) as the normal speed. In this case, however, the pitches of the descant are not exactly the same as the chorus, and so is not true augmentation. But the effect of creating a new twist to the fading chorus is the same as in a classical piece.

GHOST IN THE MACHINE

In June 1981, The Police finally finished their unprecedented world tour and met, exhausted, for yet more recording sessions on the Caribbean island of Montserrat. The *Ghost in the Machine* sessions featured more extended jams, many of which had to be shortened out of necessity (an LP record in the early 1980s could hold around 50 minutes with decent sound quality). Nevertheless, the jamming element of this album is unmistakable. Perhaps as a result of more experimentation with musical structure on the just-finished tour, the band members felt more at ease with opening up and letting loose on their respective instruments. Sting's songwriting was also more open-ended and allowed room for extended sections. "Too Much Information," "Demolition Man," and "One World" are good examples of this style. I would also characterize this album as The Police's "choral" album. Practically every song features multi-tracked vocals, all by Sting. There are also many more saxophone sounds on this album than any previously, and the synthesizer is a prominent sound as well on many songs. The album as a whole benefited from the successful production values of Hugh Padgham, who had just worked on Phil Collins's first solo effort, *Face Value*.

Partially because of the success of its first single "Every Little Thing She Does Is Magic," the album reached No. 2 on the Billboard album charts. That single made it all the way up to No. 3, setting a new record for the band. It is a rarity among Police songs: a sweet, romantic love song. However, it also presents a harmonic and musical structure that is quite sophisticated. The central musical conflict in the song is between D major and d minor, meaning that the music takes alternating notes from both those scales. The song begins with an ascending whole-tone scale fragment (a scale that is entirely made up of whole-steps between each note, as opposed to a mixture of whole and half-steps as in a typical major scale): G-A-B-C♯. At this point, we are unsure about what key the song is in. This happens over Copeland's wonderful reggae beat and Summers's constant sixteenth-note guitar part. At the end of the verse, the C♯ is finally resolved up to D, providing an exciting "answer" to the question posed in the first part of the verse. It also harmonically resolves the implied dissonance of the bass line. After a crescendo on three repeated chords under Sting's last note of the verse, he leads the chorus in with the title of the song. In this song we hear the first clue that the band is in the Caribbean: the addition of steel drums in the chorus background. I am not sure if they are synthesized or real, but whatever the case, it gives the chorus a carefree and fun feel.

At the end of the chorus is one of Sting's deft harmonic strokes. To lead back into the verse, instead of simply returning to the G-A-B-C♯ bass line, he inserts two chords that are borrowed from d minor (B♭ and F/C) and begins the G pattern with a g *minor* chord instead of G major. This may not seem significant at the time, but it proves to be so after the second chorus. Here we stay on the B♭ chord (and essentially stay in d minor) to usher in the middle of the song. This section starts with the repeated bass line of B♭-A-G-A, which halfway through gets "flipped" (or inverted) to become G-A-B♭-A. This leads smoothly into the repeated pair of B♭-C chords, over which Sting sings "When my silent fears have gripped me . . ." The last repetition creates the chord pattern of B♭-C-D, which is ubiquitous in pop and rock music of the latter twentieth century, but here it catches one off guard with how smoothly it is integrated into the song. Remember, the windup to the first chorus was approached by a bass note of C♯ (creating a half-step relationship), and here the chorus is approached by a whole step, or C-D. This borrowing of the B♭, C, and F chords from d minor continues throughout the extended coda. The harmony always returns to the D major "magic," no matter what. It is almost as if Sting is singing a love song to harmony and the tonal system itself. The "magic" is the music.

The words evoke a similar speaker to the one in "De Do Do Do": a socially awkward male who has trouble communicating with the woman he desires. It is essentially fear that "grips" him, even before he can pick up the phone to call her. Another point of contrast works well in this song: The middle section discussed above, while harmonically contrasting, also describes the speaker's resolution to call her up "a thousand times a day" and propose to her. In other words, just as the music repeatedly arrives back at D major, so the speaker repeatedly (since he states that he's done this before) lets his fears overtake him and he cannot speak to her.

This song resides in a place of infatuation from afar; a kind of adolescent lust that many of us have experienced. It is almost as if the speaker's shyness and awkwardness is protecting him, and actually talking to the woman would destroy the mystique and allure of her, thus shattering his defenses and essentially forcing him to grow up. Similarly, the harmonic world of this D major song is under attack by the "real" world of d minor. This dilemma is most clearly exhibited in the coda, with its alternating D major (on "magic") and d minor. Eventually, the music does settle into D major, with Sting's bass recalling the C♯ of the opening ascending scale figure as well as a recall of the "big enough umbrella" of the second verse.[9] When read in this way, the speaker (and the song itself) does not want to grow up, doesn't want to leave the safe space of D major.

One of the "jam" songs on *Ghost in the Machine* is "Demolition Man," also the first track recorded for the album. Perhaps more than any other Police song, "Demolition Man" takes its rhythm equally from reggae and rock. The reggae pattern that Copeland mostly uses is the "steppers" style of reggae beats (with bass drum hits on every quarter note), but he does not limit himself to that groove at all. Indeed, this track could function as a virtual catalog of the multiple ways a drummer can subdivide a four-beat measure.

Multi-tracked saxophones are featured prominently, as Sting's floating, three-chord motive hovers over the jam session. The bass riff is relentless and unchanging. It also runs the risk of becoming monotonous, stated as it is over four bars and repeated for the entire six-minute song. Sting avoids this in the chorus by actually displacing the vocal line one measure. The bass riff starts with G-A-G-A (and ends with the C-D to A in the fourth measure), but the vocal line begins during the last measure of the pattern. Both the chorus vocal line and the bass riff are the same length, so the vocals likewise end a measure before the bass riff does. The expectations have already been established by the relatively clear-cut and regular verses (and the norms of popular music phrasing), which makes the chorus that much more surprising. At the end of the chorus, it sounds as if the band is out of synch with itself, or that they have stretched the bass riff to five measures somehow without anyone noticing. But with careful listening, one can hear the completely regular and unchanging pattern of the bass against the syncopated and jumping chorus rhythms.

And of course, metaphorically it all makes sense. This is a song about spite and the destruction of a relationship. In the same way, the rhythmic energy of Copeland's drumming, the rhythmic displacement (and deliberate confusion) of Sting's vocals, and Summers's harsh and wailing guitar work throughout all give voice to the impulse to destroy. By the end, the song practically destroys itself.

Synchronicity
to Superstardom

In early 1983, after yet another world tour supporting *Ghost in the Machine,* The Police returned to Montserrat to begin recording their fifth album. The studio in question, Air Studios (founded by George Martin), was unfortunately destroyed by Hurricane Hugo in September 1989 and subsequently burned by the eruption of the Montserrat volcano in 1995. This eruption decimated the capital city of Plymouth and led the government to declare the entire southern half of the island an "exclusion zone." (Sting performed on the George Martin–organized benefit concert "Music for Montserrat" in 1997.)

As the title of this chapter suggests, the years 1983–84 saw a phenomenal rise in popularity for The Police. Wherever the line is in the popular imagination between the states of "stardom" and "superstardom," The Police crossed it in the summer of 1983. And since Sting had long been the glamorous de facto spokesman (albeit not without grumblings from his bandmates), he was placed on an even higher pedestal than before. Naturally, this led some critics to begin to despise him and others to loathe him even more. Superstardom also brought with it annoying attention from the tabloids and, on the more serious side, anonymous kidnapping threats against his children. The subject of the inevitable tradeoffs that fame brings is normally not part of a study such as this one. However, it is relevant to Sting's autobiographical output and his family's choice of residence.

Apparently the recording sessions were rather rancorous[1] but nonetheless produced their finest and most coherent album to date. Once again, Padgham provided clean and crisp production. While originally recorded in analog, many digital synthesizer effects were used (including the opening repeated pattern of "Synchronicity I"), primary among them those from the Synclavier. Sting described this early computer-aided sequencing synth as an "ideal instrument" for him.[2] Other instruments that give the album its innovative sound are Sting's saxophones, Copeland's mallet-controlled synth, and assorted exotic percussion (especially on "Walking in Your Footsteps" and "Wrapped around Your Finger"), and Summers's guitar synthesizer effects. The reggae element has been almost completely expunged, only obliquely appearing in such drum patterns as on "King of Pain," "Wrapped around Your Finger," "Tea in the Sahara," and "Murder by Numbers." The influence is rather remote and doesn't sound that exotic to twenty-first-century ears, which I believe is testament to Copeland's influence on the world of popular music drumming since The Police's success.

The Police released *Synchronicity* in June 1983, and it became their first Billboard No. 1 album. The first single (and possibly Sting's most famous song), "Every Breath You Take," held the No. 1 spot for eight weeks. Several other singles did very well ("Synchronicity II," "Wrapped around Your Finger," "King of Pain"), keeping the album in the top spot for a near record seventeen weeks.

My discussion of *Synchronicity* begins with the third track, "O My God." I feel that even though it was not a single, it is one of the strongest songs on the album, and its jazzy feel points forward to Sting's later work with the Blue Turtles band. Moreover, it has a very serious topic underneath the surface levity and the playfulness of its jazz-pop idiom. "O My God" was allegedly a reworking of an earlier song that the band only played live under the title "Three O'clock Shot."[3] The new words illustrate the gulf between God and humans, both believers and non-believers. It is a skeptic's song and seems in line with Sting's own ambivalent feelings about religion and spirituality. The phrase (or cliché) "oh my God" is said so frequently by many English-speakers that its meaning gets lost from overuse. Sting takes that ubiquitous phrase and treats it literally and creates a rich lyric that questions the idea of a loving deity. His favorite theme of loneliness comes up, as does a somewhat self-centered narrator. But if one interprets it as a prayer (granted, an anguished one) it makes perfect sense that the speaker is focused on himself.

In the last verse, the focus widens to reveal the constant inequities in the world, the imbalance of rich and poor. This relates to earlier songs with a rich/poor theme, such as "Driven to Tears" and "Invisible Sun." The reference to "turning the other cheek" is to Matthew 5:39 and has long been a problematic teaching of Jesus, though of great relevance to the idea of non-violent resistance espoused by Gandhi and Martin Luther King Jr. In this song, the skeptical speaker already has a wounded "other cheek" and so feels that it is impossible to remain passive. Perhaps it is the impetus for the song, and by extension, the prayer.

In the coda (as alluded to in the previous chapter), we have the first instance in his catalogue of Sting quoting himself in text. This passage is the text of the second verse of "Every Little Thing," which was of course about love and infatuation. In that song, the speaker expresses frustration over the apparent lack of concern of the woman for his "getting wet" during their walks in the rain. Here, the relationship is not between man and woman, but between humans and the Divine. It is fitting that the speaker is impatient or annoyed with God for his (or her) apparent lack of concern for the speaker's situation and the human condition in general. In short, Sting takes this originally playful couplet from a love song and turns it into an impassioned, frustrated plea to the Almighty. We will visit yet further contexts for this favorite stanza of Sting's.

The music underpins and underscores the speaker's ambivalence regarding God and religion. One of the few Police songs that fade in, this introduction implies that the listener is "dropping in" on a song that has been going on for some time. Considering the subject matter (religion), the implication seems to be that this kind of prayer has been said by doubting believers for centuries, and that it will continue. The bass riff sets up the song's central conflict: a confident, bluesy groove that belies the anger in the words. It is confident, perhaps, because the speaker knows what he wants from God: to fill the space between them and cure him of his loneliness. In any case, the opening riff (along with Summers's chiming harmonics) is in retrospect associated with the words "fill it up."

The verses introduce a new bass pattern, the slides and scoops showing off Sting's use of his fretless bass. The bass pattern itself includes a minor third at the top, which is the same interval between the first two "changes" (or chord pattern), a and c. This pair of notes also appears in the bass pattern of the next change (on the words "Take the space between us")—d-a-c—before returning to the home chord of a. It is intentionally ambiguous (and a typical feature of the blues) as to whether this song is in a minor or major key, since the sax and guitar parts seem to imply A major, while the chord changes (specifically on C) imply a minor. This ambiguity is a prominent feature of the opening bass riff discussed above: C and C♯ are stated right next to each other.

Two more points of articulation are worth mentioning: The first time the opening riff appears after the faded-in introduction happens at the end of the second verse, with a recall of the chorus words "fill it up." Here, Copeland really lets fly with the return of the bass riff, after a somewhat restrained introduction and two verses. It is one of my favorite moments on *Synchronicity*, displaying the band's cohesion at the top of their game.

The coda of this song I find fascinating. If this is a prayer, this is hardly a respectful "Amen." After the recall of the "Every Little Thing" lyric, we land inexplicably on F♯, and Sting plays the verse's bass pattern in that foreign key. The sax parts wail mournfully and dissonantly, while the harmonic underpinning dissolves as the bass and guitar fade away, leaving a wild duet between sax and drums. Eventually the drums also fade and we are left with a questioning, inconclusive solo saxophone.

The third single from this enormously successful album (the others being "Every Breath You Take," "King of Pain," and "Wrapped around Your Finger"),

"Synchronicity II," is one of their hardest-rocking singles. It of course is related to the opening song but also to the album's overarching theme of synchronicity, a philosophical and psychological concept first proposed by Swiss psychologist Carl Gustav Jung. While not a concept album in the literal sense, most of the songs (particularly Sting's) deal with or indirectly refer to this central idea. Jung's concept has been, in the popular imagination anyway, largely misunderstood and given more mystique than its author intended. The term does not connote, contrary to popular belief, a mysterious connection between two simultaneous but unrelated events, thus denying the possibility of coincidence. Synchronicity actually means the perception of these events as being connected; and by extension, our reaction to these simultaneous occurrences.[4] It is also related to an idea from the *I Ching* in Chinese philosophy, namely that things that happen at the same time are thus connected precisely because they are simultaneous. In a way, this idea is a bit more mundane than most people, including quite possibly Sting himself, believe. Certainly the quasi-mystical lyrics of "Synchronicity I" would attest to this.

A musically more interesting song than the opener, "Synchronicity II" uses harmonic key areas to represent, as I propose, three different elements of the lyric. After the introductory f♯ minor chord (which I will deal with below), the main part of the verse, with its sardonic snapshot of suburban life, is solidly in the key of A major. This key area connotes the "real world" of the main character, "Daddy," an overworked mid-level executive in some sort of nondescript workplace. Each of the three verses describes a specific time and locale in this real world. Verse one is "Another suburban family morning," verse two is a morning, possibly the same one, at the workplace, while the last verse is set in the evening at home (or on the way home). At the same time, or synchronously, the choruses that happen after each verse (beginning with the line "Many miles away") describe a monster emerging from the bottom of a dark Scottish lake. This section is, by contrast, in the key of a minor. Each time the chorus comes back, the monster is closer to the "real world," eventually appearing as a "shadow on the door" of a lakeside cottage.

Sting's use of the word "shadow" here is significant. Another groundbreaking idea of Jung's is the archetypal components of every individual. These five components include the self, the ego, the persona, the shadow, and the anima/animus (depending on the gender of the person; anima is the feminine part in men and animus is the corollary masculine part of women). The "shadow" of the self is essentially its opposite, a sort of anti-personality that exists within each of us. The goal of self-realization, what Jung called "individuation," is to engage with and acknowledge this shadow self, to come to terms with it and to learn to live with it.[5]

The monster in "Synchronicity II" seems to play the role of Daddy's shadow-self, which threatens to rise to the surface of his unconscious mind (the lake) and attack the cottage (a stand-in for his home life). Daddy appears to be on the brink of a major psychological episode, which, as scary as they can be for some people (sometimes leading to trauma, divorce, violence, or worse) is in fact necessary and healthy, in the long run, for the state of one's soul.

The f♯ minor opening section mentioned earlier represents this potential breakdown (or "breakthrough," as psychologists call it). This chord also appears as a mid-song "break" between the second chorus and the final verse. The harmonic contrast between the verses and choruses is not the only telling difference. The melodic and harmonic motion of the verse is generally ascending, especially evident in the initial vocal line of each verse, but also detectable in the rising harmony of A up to E at the end of the verses. Like a balancing counterweight, the chorus melody and harmony descend from A down to E, perfectly representing the complementary shadow self of the main character. So the major mode "real world" rises up to E, and the minor mode shadow world of the monster falls down to E, and the two worlds meet on this chord. This is also the chord of the coda of this song (extended from the last chorus), implying that these two worlds have met and that psychological change is possible. Summers's ascending and descending chords in this section over the sustained E bass note also suggest a sort of temporary resolution (or at least a conflation) of the two directions of up and down.

The other songs on *Synchronicity* feature more of Sting's maturing songcraft but in the interest of space will only be discussed briefly here. "Every Breath You Take" is, on the surface at any rate, a beautiful love song. The musical style, with its fairly traditional chord progression and melodic treatment, make this view easy to understand. Those who delve deeper into the lyrical content, however, find a song sung from the viewpoint of an embittered, angry ex-lover. The only harmonic shift away from the home key of A major happens in the "middle 8" (here, actually the "middle 10"), when we briefly "borrow" two chords from a minor (F and G). This musical departure makes sense, as the speaker for the first time addresses the past, talking about what has happened since the break-up ("Since you've gone I've been lost without a trace"). This is the only glimpse we get into the speaker's psychology other than the constant thoughts of retribution, stalking, and revenge. It's interesting that Sting seems to enjoy subverting stylistic tropes through the lyrical subject matter. In earlier songs, he used the tropes of rock and reggae to sing about loneliness and rhetorical suicide, and here he mimics a love song to broach the subject of bitterness and obsession.

"King of Pain," the second top-10 single from this album (peaking at No. 3 on the Billboard charts), operates on a similar level as the previous songs. It is, once again, an up-tempo, nice-sounding song about fairly dark subject matter. "King of Pain" was originally conceived of by Sting as a pun on "King of Spain." As he has stated, he often conceives of a title first and builds a lyric around that. The music usually is composed at the same time as part of the same process. In general terms, "King of Pain" might be thought of as simply death, or perhaps the devil, in various guises.

This song has one of the largest sonic compasses on the album, ranging from pure silence on the one hand to full pop orchestration on the other. It also varies in mood, from forlorn and empty to accepting and determined. These emotional areas correspond musically with the relative keys of b minor and D major. I feel that Summers could have done more with the guitar solo, as here he simply imitates the verse melody. Copeland, however, provides a constantly fascinating variation of drum patterns, culminating in off-beat bass drum hits in the last verse.

This album is full of literary references, including the Faust legend in "Wrapped around Your Finger" and Paul Bowles's novel *The Sheltering Sky* in "Tea in the Sahara." "Murder by Numbers" takes the apparently innocuous world of drawing-room murder mysteries a la Agatha Christie's Miss Marple and extends the metaphor out to genocide and nuclear annihilation. This album was a product of its time, the early 1980s, and certainly the looming threat of nuclear conflict between the United States and the USSR was a pervasive fear for many. "Walking in Your Footsteps" (the only non-single from the album to be included on the 2007 reunion tour), uses the extinction of the dinosaurs as an allegory for our own potential destruction and asks the question, "Are we following the same path?"

Synchronicity was, in many respects, the pinnacle of the three men's careers. And at the time it seemed that the Police were unstoppable. During the subsequent extremely long (nine months) and grueling world tour, Sting apparently decided that this was it. This was as far as he wanted to go with this band. Nothing was really permanently decided, and the band had even begun to record their sixth studio album in the spring of 1986. Personal conflict between the three, particularly Sting and Copeland, coupled with a polo injury to Copeland resulted in only one song being completed ("Don't Stand So Close to Me '86"), which none of the band were happy with. This rather anemic single simply became the selling point of a greatest hits collection.

The great Police, Stewart's band, had folded and gone out on top of the world in a blaze of red, yellow, and blue. Meanwhile, Sting's dream of becoming a solo artist had been brewing for years in the secret places of his heart. This dream would wake him up.

Going Solo

On March 4, 1984, The Police played their final show of the typically exten-
sive and globetrotting *Synchronicity* tour in Melbourne, Australia. Sting at
that point had tired of the constant write, record, tour pattern of the past
seven years. He had reportedly been vocal about it backstage after one of the
shows at New York's Shea Stadium.[1] The tension between members of the
band had reached unworkable levels. Each of the three men normally traveled separately to the next show, had separate dressing rooms, and really only
saw each other onstage during sound checks and performances. They were
splintering as a group and had been, slowly, for some time.

It seems to be a pattern in the break-up of many bands since The Beatles in
the late 1960s that one or more members start embarking on solo projects.
Sting did just that, although modestly at first and not really intending to
launch a solo career, with the release of the *Brimstone & Treacle* soundtrack.
An unlikely hit single in the UK, "Spread a Little Happiness" reached No. 1
on the charts. The song was used as the end title music in a very ironic way,
since Sting's character Martin was a con man, thief, and rapist. The song was
originally from a 1929 musical called "Mr. Anders" by Vivian Ellis (1904–
1996), Clifford Grey, and G. Newman.[2] The British public really connected
with the wryness of Sting's tongue-in-cheek vocal trills and stylistic incongru-
ity. Although the nostalgia-filled style of British popular music from between
the wars was very unlike anything Sting had ever sung with The Police, it
was somewhat closer to the style of music that he was playing while with the
Newcastle Big Band: jazz standards and big band charts from the 1930s and
1940s. Perhaps this tangential result of his acting career, coming three years

before he actually struck out on his own, planted (or reinvigorated) the seeds of becoming a solo artist. Another solo performance from 1982 that raised some eyebrows was his acoustic rendition of "Message in a Bottle" during the *Secret Policeman's Other Ball,* a musical variety-type show organized by members of Monty Python.

THE DREAM OF THE BLUE TURTLES

It was a dream that he had, however, that spurred him on to form a new backing band of some of the finest jazz musicians of the mid-1980s. He dreamt of turtles that kept hanging out in his garden, crawling around and munching on various green leafy plants. The surreal dreamlike element was that these turtles happened to be enormous and blue.[3] They wouldn't leave no matter what he tried. As any reader of Jung would be, he was fascinated by the symbolism in this dream. Who were these blue turtles, and why were they destroying his garden?

As he told the *Los Angeles Times* in June 1985, "The turtle is a creature who lives both under the sea and out of it. The sea is a good symbol of the subconscious."[4] Eventually he decided that it had to do with his career and that the turtles were symbols of this new band that he needed to form. Whatever one makes of the turtles as symbols, they become significant for us as listeners because Sting interpreted them as one reason to change direction in his musical life. "There is no greater risk than this project," he told Vic Garbarini.[5]

During much of 1984, Sting wrote and created demo tracks (using his Synclavier) of the songs for what would become his first solo album, *The Dream of the Blue Turtles.* Some of the melodies (specifically "We Work the Black Seam") were very old and had just been waiting for the right time and medium in which to emerge. Others like "Shadows in the Rain" and, eventually, "Bring on the Night" were reworkings or reimaginings of Police songs. Sting decided that the best way to form his band was to hire jazz musicians because they would potentially have the discipline to work within a prescribed song structure but also the fluidity and freedom to be themselves within that structure. He also may have thought that a jazz musician would naturally be more able to take direction from a "band leader," unlike the strong personalities that made up The Police. However, throughout the process of making *The Dream of the Blue Turtles* and its subsequent tour, Sting insisted that this was not really a "solo" album, and not a "jazz" album.

Through his record label (still A&M) he was introduced to Branford Marsalis, a young member of the burgeoning jazz renaissance of the 1980s and also the oldest brother of the Marsalis jazz dynasty. Sting and Marsalis hit it off immediately and have remained close friends ever since. Sting received many recommendations for other players from Marsalis, including keyboardist Kenny Kirkland, another major figure in Sting's solo career. For some positions, like the bass and drums, he held invited auditions in New York. From these he selected Darryl Jones, a bassist who had been recently playing with Miles Davis, and drummer Omar Hakim, formerly with the fusion band Weather Report.

A significant decision that Sting made in the creation of this album is that the newly formed band would learn the new songs, perform a few shows live, and then record the album. In doing this, he hoped to foster the kind of brotherly and musical connections that he once enjoyed over the many years of touring with The Police. The new band made its world debut at the Ritz Theater in New York on February 25, 1985. The three-night stand was then assessed later in the studio during the recording of the album. Undoubtedly, changes were made in some of the songs. It is hard to know without listening to a bootleg recording of the Ritz shows.

In a further departure from his working methods with The Police, Sting presented the new band with self-produced demo versions of most of the songs for the new album, with the exception of "Love Is the Seventh Wave," which was composed in the studio during recording. The studio in question was (to continue Sting's habit of recording in the Caribbean) Eddy Grant's facility on Barbados. For these demos, Sting once again relied on the Synclavier (as well as other sequencing synthesizers and drum machines) to create them. The result was that Sting as a solo artist exerted more control over the composition of the basic structure of the songs than he had with The Police, where some compositional decisions were undoubtedly more collective in nature. Of course, some Police songs were "presented" by Sting to the band as demos ("Every Little Thing" for example), but Summers and Copeland had more freedom in their response to them.

The opening track, also the first single from the new album, "If You Love Somebody Set Them Free" immediately signals a departure from *Synchron-icity*'s dark Jung-laden pop/rock. The song sets the tone of the album stylistically in the sense that this song collection will be a skilled and pleasing mélange of styles. This is in fact what I feel to be the hallmark of Sting's solo career: a postmodern use of musical style as signifier in order to convey the message of the song. Sting's stylistic umbrella as a composer is big enough for a multitude of musics.

In the case of "If You Love Somebody," Sting recalls 1960s Motown and Stax Records-style gospel-tinged rhythm and blues. The only thing it *lyrically* has in common with that music, however, is the subject of love. This is not a typical "love song," even though the subject of the song is in fact love. Sting very rarely writes a straight-ahead love song ("Every Little Thing" being the obvious standout) but typically explores a myriad of other topics under the umbrella of love. This fondness for redefining the love song continued right up until the most recent song (at the time of this writing) in his catalogue, "Sacred Love." So "If You Love Somebody" is an ideal example of the use of a style often associated with the love song and Sting's ability to expand upon the idea, creating a much richer musical, lyrical, and stylistic tapestry of associations.

The song speaks of the early stages of a relationship, the one in which some lovers can feel possessive about the other, often leading to suspicion and jealousy. Sting's exhortation of "set them free" is initially presented as a paradox: Normally we think of a husband, girlfriend, or lover as "mine." And "that's all some people ever want to be." But Sting's point is that real love is about freedom; freedom with limits. Trying to possess someone as an object is not healthy and is not love, but it is detrimental to the souls of both parties. The "middle" (third) stanza alludes to this. We are taught by tradition, by capitalism, by some religions, that we must always want more of everything. Accumulation of wealth is the goal, and Sting makes the scary connection that sometimes this tendency is to accumulate people too: "Everything we see, we want to possess."

This middle eight is in the contrasting key of C major (the majority of the song is in d Dorian). This works not only as an effective musical contrast but also serves to "set off" these lines as the major point of the song. The chorus is somewhat similarly treated, with its sudden shift upwards in the vocal and change of mode to the suggestion of D major. The song never permanently changes key, however, as it reverts back to the opening riff on the words "set them free," solidly in d minor (Dorian).

Since this is the first new song most Sting fans had heard in two years, it is worth mentioning the expanded sonic palette. First of all, this first single was very different from the synthesizer-drenched sound of most mid-1980s singles. The song's prominent instrumental colors were that of the Hammond B-3 organ, the tambourine, and the funk bass of Darryl Jones. The Synclavier can only be heard about halfway through the song in the contrasting middle eight. While the sound itself was not "new" per se, since it borrowed heavily from gospel music and rhythm and blues, the combination was new: Sting making music with black jazz musicians, singing a sophisticated song about love that is not a love song.

Personally, I distinctly remember hearing this song for the first time in my parent's old VW bus, having just learned to drive and parking in front of the Riverside Public Library in my sunny California hometown. I couldn't leave the car until I heard the new song. Of course I knew it was Sting, but what was he singing? Gospel? Was that a tambourine? After the initial internal readjustment to this new phase of his career, I decided I liked it and bounded up the library steps.

The next track of the new album, "Love Is the Seventh Wave" continues the stylistic mélange while hearkening back to The Police's early use of overt reggae beats. The difference here is that this new song is exceedingly optimistic and in a major key, while many of The Police's reggae tracks were in the minor mode (the standout exception is "So Lonely"). This song was really collectively composed by the band; it came out of a reggae jam session in the studio. The next day, Sting came back with lyrics and a melody.[6] This "free" style of composition is evident in the playful nature of the words as the song fades with a parody of "Every Breath You Take": "Every cake you bake/Every leg you break." Along with the "big enough umbrella" couplet, this is another favorite self-parody of Sting's.

Musically, the song is simple. Similar to many songs written by Bob Marley, "Love Is the Seventh Wave" is really centered on one chord. The vocals decorate the chord somewhat, but they always return to the home chord of G major. This is a song that shows off Sting's melodic gifts very well. Over an essentially unchanging harmonic backdrop, the vocal melody provides enough variety over the course of 3 1/2 minutes to keep the listener engaged. Another way Sting achieves this variety is through sectional contrasts. After the third chorus (which, incidentally, has the same harmonic progression as the verse), Branford Marsalis takes a long-breathed solo that adds new pitches to the mix. Verse three sees the addition of backing harmony vocals and Sting's Synclavier pattern. Later, verse five is sung in an "a cappella" style (although with drums), serving to heighten the seriousness of the apocalyptic words at that point.

Sting based this song on the surfer's secret that the seventh wave in a succession of ocean waves is the best one to surf. He heard this from local people during the *Blue Turtle* sessions on Barbados. Sting takes this idea and applies it to waves of ideas and proposes that all previous waves will be washed away by the seventh, which will be stronger, deeper, and unstoppable, and which is love. The beauty of this lyric is that the word love (the subject of the song) doesn't appear until the very end. This type of poetic tradition is as old as poetry itself: the use of symbol and metaphor to describe a concept. In this case, withholding the idea itself explicitly until the end makes the listener engage more fully with the subject.

This song, like the album's opening, is also about love. But one would hardly consider this a "love song." It is about universal love: love between cultures and countries and thus a vision of world peace. It may seem cliché, but the true polarity is not between good and evil but between love and fear; between love and the absence of love. This ties in with Sting's essentially humanist view of the world.

The shadow of the cold war seems to pervade this album. With the nuclear arms race between the United States and the USSR in full swing in 1985, Western Europe was in the crosshairs. The United States used West Germany and other European countries as launching pads for various short-range missiles. This was ostensibly to protect Western Europe from attack, but many Europeans felt that the silos were targets and thus made their citizens more vulnerable. This constant fear and ambivalence towards the United States is palpable in the song "Russians," the third track on this album.

An unlikely hit single because of its absence of a traditional drum sound and its heavy subject matter, it peaked at No. 16 on the Billboard chart in

February 1986. Listeners likely resonated with the fear of nuclear war, mixed with the hope that the Soviets are humans, too: the hope that in the interest of keeping their children alive they would not want a nuclear conflict. In the twenty-first century this seems a rather obvious statement, but during the cold war (just as in any war) the level of propaganda was high, and there was a general stereotype in the West of Russians as one-dimensional communist automatons.

Although some of the rhymes are forced, the message of the song is honest and direct. Cutting through all the political rhetoric on both sides of the Iron Curtain, the essential fact remains that "we share the same biology" and thus have the capacity to love our children just as much as our supposed enemies do. Once again, as in "Love Is the Seventh Wave," the universally shared aspects of love have the potential to save the world.

This time, however, the mood is dark and heavy. We enter into this ominous soundscape by way of a ticking clock (which turns out to set the tempo of the song using sixteenth notes), and anonymous voices speaking in English and Russian. German writer Christian Jahl has noted that the left channel contains a Russian voice and the right an English one.[7] This introduction creates a sense of urgency, with the voices creating a kind of "broadcast" quality, and the ticking of the clock implies that we as humans don't have much time left.

Sting originally (and naively) wanted to record "Russians" in the Soviet Union with an actual Russian orchestra.[8] He quickly realized that in the mid-1980s this would be impossible. Nevertheless, he kept the quasi-orchestral sound in Kirkland's synthesized woodwind and string mix. Much of this orchestral conception comes from Sting's use of a melody by Sergei Prokofiev (1891–1953) from a suite of incidental music written for the film *Lieutenant Kije* (1933). The film tells the satirical story of an imaginary officer in the tsarist army who was accidentally created by a slip of the pen on an official document. Rather than admit their mistake to the imposing tsar, his subordinates invent an entire life for Kije: He is born, falls in love, gets married, gets drunk, goes on a sleigh ride, and eventually has to die before the tsar can meet him. The tune Sting chose is the "Romance" section, which in the original Prokofiev is first presented as a double bass solo. This may have been the initial attraction to the tune, but more likely Sting happened upon it through his admiration for Prokofiev's music and his interest in Prokofiev's *Peter and the Wolf*. He eventually provided narration for a recording of the work conducted by Claudio Abbado in 1993. Subsequently he appeared in a puppet version made for television.[9] Another possible connection that could be made is between Sting's public persona and the completely fictitious officer, Lt. Kije. Could Sting have seen a bit of himself in that wholly invented character?

A feature of "Russians" worth noting is that Sting's treatment of the Prokofiev melody is more "classical" (or more accurately, "Baroque") than the original. The harmony feels more "filled out" and complete and includes chords that are not in the Prokofiev. In fact, the chord progression underneath the borrowed tune is what Sting uses to form the foundation of the verse melody. The verses are loosely based on the "Romance" tune but could really function more like a countermelody to it. This is why the Prokofiev tune seems fully integrated into the song: It is not grafted on as an afterthought to simply give the song some kind of legitimacy; rather it is an integral part of the music.

The gloomy mood continues in the next song, "Children's Crusade." The overarching theme once again is love and war and the absence of love during war. The wars referred to in this song are the so-called Children's Crusade of the thirteenth century, World War I, and the heroin crisis in Britain in the 1980s. Sting's anger is justly directed at those people in power who either allowed or caused these young men to die: the Catholic Church, the British military and government, and the drug cartels involved in international opium trafficking, respectively. Sting does not specifically address the Children's Crusade but uses it as a metaphoric connective theme between WWI and the present day (1984).

The events of the early thirteenth century have for the most part been inflated and exaggerated. For example, there were accounts of boys having visions of marching to Jerusalem and peacefully converting the Muslim population after parting the waters of the Mediterranean. Most scholars now believe that the people who did band together and migrate in the general direction of Jerusalem were simple groups of roving poor, called "pueri" by monks whose hospitality they sought. These people had been misplaced by economic hardship and war in Central Europe. "Pueri" simply meant "boys" in Latin, but this word was most likely mistranslated over the centuries into "children." This group or groups of poverty-stricken nomads (of all ages) were probably captured and simply sold into slavery as soon as they got to Italy. There have been several works of fiction, poetry, art, and film that have perpetuated the legend and embellished the few facts that are certifiable.

Given this, it is plain that Sting's historical view is much more based on the facts available. The British experience during World War I, while initially full of great national pride and a sense of optimism, soon became characterized by the futility of trench warfare and the deadlock of 1916–17. A mandatory draft was instituted in 1916. As a result of the folly of specific campaigns (the Dardandelles, Salonika) and general mismanagement of the war on the ground, over half of an entire generation of British young men lost their lives: 750,000 killed and 2,500,000 wounded.[10] It was a poorly managed and poorly fought war that ended with the dissolution of the British Empire and a disastrous treaty that contributed to the rise of Hitler 14 years later.

While not directly analogous to the young men being drafted and sent off to war to die, the drug problem does also largely affect the poor and unemployed. Heroin, a drug derived from opium, is extremely addictive, and thus its users become "opium slaves," as Sting writes. Opium is produced from poppies, which for Sting is the connective thematic tissue between these two historical moments, as the poppy is still symbolically worn in England on Remembrance Day (November 11, formerly Armistice Day, commemorating the end of World War I. It is similar to the American Veterans' Day). The tradition of poppy wearing is at least as old as a poem by John McCrae (1872–1918) called "In Flanders Fields," written in 1915. McCrae was a Canadian physician who attended the dying during the battle of Ypres. The poem was first published in *Punch* and became extremely popular both during and after the war. It is McCrae's only well-known poem.

With such a rich background for the text, one expects an equally rich musical fabric to accompany it. Sting delivers. It is a song with a wide range of dynamics, from the quiet opening three-note keyboard figure, to the wailing and screaming of Marsalis' extended soprano sax solo in the central section, back down to the recall of the three-note motive at the very end, this time with a dissonant fourth note (A♯ over an E bass.) This final keyboard motive feels like the "answer" to the question posed by the opening melody. Instead of resolution, however, the question is answered by another question.

Harmonically, "Children's Crusade" is very sophisticated. In fact, the "home" key is ambiguous until the very end (it is e minor). But, because the verses start on and seem to be in the key of b minor, the listener is led to believe that this is the key of the whole song. The only significant section that uses e minor extensively is the sax solo. I think that Sting uses this harmonic structure for a reason: to make a musical and metaphoric connection between the hell of battle and the central concept of the song, the sacrifice of the young for the profit and power of the old. The repetitive, swirling sax solo is punctuated by horrific synthesizer swells from Kirkland, in which one can practically see the "Children of England . . . dying in waves." Marsalis's solo climaxes with the final synthesizer wave, and we get the final chorus, lustily sung by a multi-tracked Sting with his characteristic countermelodies and harmonies. But the hell of the e minor is still in our ears.

In the final verse, the music returns to the earlier, calmer volume level to address the contemporary drug problem in Britain. Here, Sting plays on the meaning of the word "trade": used in the sense of "barter" (as it was in verse two), and also as "economy"—in this case the drug trade. On the last line, "All for a Children's Crusade," we finally settle on the home key of e minor (connecting with the solo section), and the song ends with the musical question mark mentioned above.

Originally the end of side one of the LP and cassette versions, "Shadows in the Rain" is a straight-ahead rocker: a reworking of a Police track originally included on the album *Zenyatta Mondatta*. This new treatment could not be more different. The key is bumped up a step to enliven Sting's voice, the reggae beat is gone, and the overworked and rather dull echo effects have been replaced by a prominent vocal track; the whole character of the song has been changed. Sting has said that this new version is closer to his original idea of the song.[11]

The subject of "Shadows in the Rain" seems to be madness, not drug addiction as might be inferred. But the most important element of this version is the music: the unrelenting tempo, the creative drumming of Hakim, the extended structure allowing for both a keyboard solo and a sax solo. In the last chorus, Sting's characteristic "cha" shouts appear, intersecting the measures to suddenly give it a ska/white reggae feel. This musical interjection appeared in a handful of Police songs, including "Hole in My Life" and "Reggatta de Blanc."

This song is the best example of what Sting felt to be his mission for this album and possibly for his solo career as a whole: a true jazz-rock pop fusion that has enough musical space to allow for both a catchy chorus and extended solos. By reworking an old, rather anemic Police song into this jumping dance number, Sting symbolically is asserting control over his catalogue of songs and saying that he has the freedom to do what he wants with them. Songs for Sting are like storyboards: You have the sketched image of generally what the cinematographer's shot will look like, but the execution could be achieved in any number of creative ways. This explains why in live performances he almost never plays his songs in the same way from tour to tour; chords will be added, and instrumental arrangements especially are altered. The songs are alive and breathing, capable of being transformed into something new.

Another transformation into something new comes with the song "We Work the Black Seam Together," which makes a connection with the English poet William Blake (1757–1827) and his quatrain

> And did the Countenance Divine
> Shine forth upon our clouded hills?
> And was Jerusalem builded here
> Among these dark Satanic Mills? (Wm. Blake, *Preface to Milton*)

These lines were written in 1804, and Sting likely encountered them in church as a boy: This poem was set to music by Charles Hubert Parry in the late nineteenth century to create a most English national hymn, "Jerusalem." It is still sung today at occasions of national pride: Soccer matches and the final night of the BBC proms are two examples that I have encountered.

Blake's poem is about the earthly paradise that he thought England was created to be (Jerusalem); however the England of Blake's day had, in his view, been warped from this original and divine beginning. Blake was writing at the time of the Industrial Revolution (late eighteenth century), which completely changed the way of life of the British lower classes. Previously unthinkable working conditions were now a reality: long hours, seven days a week, dank and unheated factories, children working for practically no money, repetitive and unchallenging jobs. None of these conditions would find a place in Blake's version of paradise.

Sting, in his song "We Work the Black Seam," makes the connection to Blake's "Dark Satanic Mills" in reference to nuclear power plants, which in the 1970s and 1980s began replacing coal as Britain's main energy resource. The song was actually written in support of the Miner's Strike of 1984–85, which eventually was defeated and led to the break-up of the largest miner's union.[12] *The Dream of the Blue Turtles* was released several months after the strike was over, but its effects would still echo through the British labor force for the rest of the decade. As a song, "We Work the Black Seam" stands as an elegiac poem to the working class. Sting takes the struggle of a specific industry and makes it universal by focusing on themes of economic power, self-worth, and rapidly changing technology.[13]

One of the notable musical features of this song is the constant, incessant drum pattern (possibly played by a drum machine). Its prominent three eighth notes in the bass drum (surrounding beat two of every bar) bring to mind some sort of mechanized factory, constantly churning out a product. The factory never stops, which is implied by the use of the fade-in and fade-out as a frame for this song. The basic struggle implied here, then, is between humans and technology, or "man and machine." The beauty of it is that Sting creates a haunting folk music inspired song around this mechanization.

The main verse tune was actually written several years before, during Sting's Last Exit days. Sting has said that it was one of those melodies that hang around in his head until he matches the right lyric with it.[14] In this case, the combination of a folk-like melody with the drum machine works perfectly.

The introduction fades in, as stated above, along with Marsalis's soprano sax refrain and Kirkland's synthesizer eighth notes.[15] The synth pattern uses many "open" fifths and fourths, which are two-note chords that, because of the lack of a third, are often used to create a pale, spare quality. This old verse tune, as stated above, is inspired by English folk song. It uses a modal scale (in this case, Dorian) which is almost a minor scale but not quite. Many English and Scottish tunes use this scale, and some of those tunes are hundreds of years old, predating the establishment of the major/minor tonal system (which happened around 1700).

The melody is also notable for its additive structure. Each phrase fragment builds upon the last, until the third and final phrase makes a grand arc from the tonic note "a" up to a high "b" and back down again. The chorus melody is not as interesting structurally, but this fact gives it contrast to the verse. This fits with the future-focused chorus, "One day in a nuclear age," as opposed to the verses, which are grounded in the present. Also, as we have seen in many previous songs, Sting uses the chorus chords metaphorically as a temporary escape from the "reality" of the home key of a minor. The basic progression is: F-C-d-a, which is repeated three times. On the fourth pass, on the words "Carbon 14," the pattern stops on the d chord. This allows Kirkland and Jones to play a cascading scale down from F, leading us smoothly back to a minor and the title words of the song.

This song also features Branford Marsalis in three notable ways. Throughout this album he uses his various saxophones as commentators, responding to Sting's vocalizations. This is what he does in the verses of "We Work the Black Seam." But Marsalis also provides a crucial "refrain" figure beginning with a rising fifth. As stated earlier, this motive begins the song. It also comes back during the title words/refrain of the chorus. A third role that the sax plays is as a rising countermelody in the first part of the chorus. This line is a wonderful setup to the previously mentioned descending scale in the keyboard and bass. This "question-answer" balance metaphorically illustrates the hope that someday people will understand why the miners had a problem with the antiseptic, inhuman, and dangerous world of nuclear power. This momentary hope is then balanced by the quick descending scale tumbling back into the present, to "work the black seam together."

It is worth mentioning that this song is one of the first in Sting's catalogue to have environmentalism as a secondary topic. Increasingly in his career, but especially in the late 1980s and 1990s, he has been known as an activist for environmentalism and human rights. He and Trudie Styler (his second wife) founded the Rainforest Foundation in 1989, and The Police briefly reunited in 1986 for Amnesty International's "Conspiracy of Hope" tour. So for all the identification with the miners during the strike (and frequent self-identification as a product of the working class), a theme of this song that is equally important is that of environmental pollution. From burying the "waste in a great big hole" to the polluted streams of Cumberland (one of the largest mining districts near Newcastle), the message of environmentalism and the dangers of nuclear power is prominent throughout "We Work the Black Seam."

The dark mood continues for the next track, "Consider Me Gone." Although Sting has never acknowledged it, the song could be interpreted as referring to the break-up of The Police. However, his first marriage to Frances Tomelty had been breaking up during the dizzying year of 1983, so it could also be relevant to his divorce. In any case, the song is about the end of a relationship, fading in with the kernel of an intense argument, "You can't say that!"

In the first verse, Sting uses a house as a metaphor for a relationship. Once full of care and forgiveness, it is now barren and empty: deliberately cleared out by the people involved. The second verse paraphrases lines two through five of Shakespeare's Sonnet 35, another string of metaphors for beautiful things that have dangers or traps in them:

Roses have thorns, and silver fountains mud;
Clouds and eclipses stain both moon and sun,
And loathsome canker lives in sweetest bud.
All men make faults

Sting has switched the order of the second and third lines printed above to conform with his rhyme scheme and has added the final rhyme of "And history reeks of the wrongs we have done."

It is fascinating to interpret this self-critical, guilt-laden verse in terms of Sting's view of his own media image. A man with dashing good looks, seen as a sex symbol for many people, acknowledges that he, too, like the rose with thorns, has done wrong and has skeletons in his closet. At the same time, it is a perfect sketch of a strained relationship that is struggling to keep up appearances.

The third verse is perhaps the most revealing and autobiographical. Sting's "search for perfection," in the context of the interpretation of the second verse as centered around beauty and fame, is actually a hell that he creates for himself. Perfection for any mortal is an unattainable goal, and the pursuit of it can drive one mad. Sting may have experienced this directly during The Police's apex (and, by most accounts, he did).

A nice musical feature of "Consider Me Gone" is that each verse has a different melody based on the text of each. All three verses share an affinity for the raised fourth scale degree (in this case, G-over the home key of D♭). This interval is known as the tritone, which is one of the most dissonant intervals in the tonal system. The note can be heard in the first verse on the words "were" and "the" in the first three lines of the melody and also on the word "say" in the refrain "you can't say that." The effect that this dissonance creates is one of instability and discomfort.

The formal structure is fairly standard with alternating verses and choruses ("After today, consider me gone"), with the exception of the transition from the third verse to the final chorus. This interlude features a descending walking-bass sequence, leading down from A♭ to G♭ to F♭ (or E, the lowest note on the bass), before returning to A♭ for a climactic final chorus. Omar Hakim propels the band into a double-time feel and provides an exciting rhythmic back-and-forth between himself and Kirkland's organ. The effect is one of "moving on" with the speaker's life and out of this empty house.

Next comes the first of a handful of instrumental numbers in Sting's solo career. Many of these ended up as B-sides, and "The Dream of the Blue Turtles" is by far the most significant instrumental track in his output. As stated earlier, Sting's dream of blue turtles destroying his garden is possibly what led him on the path of his solo career.[16] The track itself is a study in contrasts, with two main musical ideas competing for prominence. A quiet, jazzy, "swung" opening melody (theme one, which again emphasizes the raised fourth scale degree),[17] alternates with straight-eighth fanfare-like music (theme two), in which the bass rather than the melody features the tritone. The central section is a wild, bebop-inspired solo by Kirkland, which is of course once again swung. For the latter half of the track, the two themes are reversed: theme two and then theme one, ending inconclusively with a chord including the recurrent tritone, amid Marsalis's mysterious laughter.

Given Sting's description of his dream, it seems logical that this tune is a musical illustration of the turtles destroying his garden. The interpretive question is this: What music represents Sting, or the garden, and what the turtles? On the one hand, the fun, carefree swung sections may represent Sting casually strolling out to his garden. The plodding tritone-based "straight" section would then signify the lumbering, destructive turtles. The central solo section could thus be interpreted as Sting trying to stop the destruction, hurriedly scampering about to no avail. The ending would then be one of frustration and non-resolution.

The counter-interpretation is perhaps more compelling. In this one, the turtles are represented by the swung, be-bop sections, and Sting (or his garden, or his seemingly well-ordered, established life) is therefore the straight-eighth fanfare theme (which has elements of British speech rhythm to it). In this reading, the swung rhythm is seen as more "natural" and "free" and even closer to the unconscious mind (hence the improvised solo is also seen as "Turtle" music). And it is the plodding, awkward, straight-eighths (in which everything is "notated") that signify Sting making a vain attempt to command the turtles to stop. In the end, the turtles win and exit the way they came, laughing as they leave the garden in ruins.

This second interpretation feels better to me, partially because it touches on the very old dichotomy of Apollo and Dionysus—two poles of human nature, artistic temperament, and society that have informed countless works of art. Apollo represents the rational, reasoned, and orderly (focused on the brain), while Dionysus represents the irrational, chaotic, and unpredictable (focused on the body). In music, this conflict has surfaced in the twentieth century with often fascinating results. Jazz is just one example of a successful hybrid between the two. More discussion of this topic is beyond the scope of this book.[18]

In both interpretations, the garden is destroyed. Sting's old way of life and making music is now gone and replaced by this new style (for him). Significantly, the track has an unstable, inconclusive ending (with a dissonant diminished chord). This matches Sting's own insecurities about this career move and formation of the new band.

But, of course, this unstable chord has a musical function as well. It serves to move the listener on to the next song, "Moon over Bourbon Street," one of the most atmospheric songs on the album. It begins with a hugely contrasting texture from the previous "busy" jazz tune: solo vocal and acoustic bass. This is the only song on the album in which Sting plays bass. For some songs throughout his career, he has preferred to use a fretless instrument, either the Ibanez fretless model or a stand-up bass with a cutaway body made by the Human Company.[19] This curious name for the company is the reason that Sting has affectionately named his stand-up bass "Brian." This instrument can be seen during "Walking on the Moon" in the *Synchronicity* concert video. A fretless bass such as this is used by many respected jazz and fusion bassists such as Stanley Jordan. It is a more challenging instrument to play because the notes are not given to the player, by sight or by feel. There are no frets that stop the string from vibrating at a predetermined spot. So the player can actually play "in between" the notes. Players must rely much more on their ears to determine pitch. Also, one is much more free to slide notes up or down the fingerboard. This can lead to quite expressive bass lines, as Sting provides on "Moon over Bourbon Street."

In this song, Sting is betraying his debt to the Tin Pan Alley songwriters of the 1920s and 30s who ushered in the "Golden Age" of Broadway (1943–1968). Echoes of Cole Porter, George Gershwin, and even Kurt Weill can be heard in the harmonic structure, the melody, and especially the instrumentation. Kirkland's keyboards throughout imitate a string orchestra; there is Sting's bass, Marsalis's soprano saxophone, and only minimal percussion from Hakim (a bass drum and hi-hat alternation.) The instrumentation itself goes a long way toward expressing the restrained, tortured feelings of the speaker of the song: Louis the Vampire.

Anne Rice's *Interview with the Vampire,* when published in 1976, was the first well-known novel to revisit the vampire legend since Bram Stoker's *Dracula*. Rice's book single-handedly reintroduced vampires into the public consciousness. Like the vampires themselves, these stories have existed for hundreds of years and are fleshed out and given contemporary contexts by various authors. Rice's Louis is a fascinating character because of his vestigial human morality, which makes his need for killing and human blood a constant source of conflict in his soul. As Sting says, "I was trapped in this life, like an innocent lamb"; Louis was attacked, bitten, and given this vampire existence by Lestat, who becomes a sort of reluctant mentor for him.

Much of the tale that Louis relates takes place in the eighteenth and nineteenth centuries, in New Orleans, Romania, and Paris. The "interview" itself takes place in present-day (or 1970s) San Francisco. This explains why Sting chose a kind of jazz/classical hybrid style for this song. The song's structure is simple: three verses alternating with an instrumental refrain, with a middle "break" before the last verse. This break is deliberately "classical" in nature and seems to describe Louis' upper-class eighteenth-century origins.

Musically, Sting is here most likely imitating the melancholic or sorrowful affect of eighteenth-century music. To denote sorrow in a musical way, composers often used a descending half-step, which imitated the sound of sobs. This gesture is easy to hear in the "Crucifixus" movement of Bach's Mass in B minor, as well as in several other opera arias of the period. In this middle section of "Moon over Bourbon Street," an oboe and English horn play a mournful melody built of this musical idea, thereby expressing the melancholy of this unwilling vampire who must kill innocent people to survive. The very last few moments of the song recall this descending half-step, before Sting's bowed bass note and a wolf howl in the distance.

Sting's first solo release ends with the second top-10 single from the album, "Fortress around Your Heart." The song peaked at No. 8 on the Billboard Hot 100 chart. It is fairly rare for a top-10 single to use the rhetorical device of allegory as heavily as Sting does in this song. The "fortress" constructed by the speaker originally to protect the lover has, ironically, now become a prison because of the battle raging all around.

In an allegory, each element of the scene or story has a specific meaning in both the allegorical world and in the real world. In this song, the city is under siege by unknown forces, with siege guns bombarding it all night. But, apparently, the fortress has survived and the occupants are safe but unable to move. The speaker says that the city was built in a day, and now he is presumably (from the opening verse) returning at night from a battle that he had "invented inside [his] head." This is the only line in the song (with the notable exception of the title) that even remotely refers to the "real world," betraying that this extended metaphor exists entirely in the realm of the imagination.

In the chorus, the speaker talks of building bridges over the chasm and burning down the battlements surrounding the fortress, thus providing freedom for the occupants of the embattled relationship. The war has really destroyed the city (or the relationship), but the fortress at the center of the city remains; in this case, the lover's heart. The speaker seems to have been gone so long that he is now seen as an outsider. This is why he needs to return under cover of darkness while the armies are sleeping. By returning, he is trying to make amends, and to do that he must set the lover's heart free.

As he returns, he recognizes the walls (in verse one), the tattered flag (verse two), and the lands and the fields where he once played (verse three). In other words, he is looking back on himself in the early part of the relationship, seeing the barriers that he put up, an almost meaningless, weathered display of their love, and seeing himself as a happier man in the past. And at the end of each verse, he reminds himself not to fall into his own traps of self-destruction (the mines).

I believe Sting's essential point in this song is that falling in love is relatively easy ("It took a day to build the city"), but that we build up so many defenses and traps around it that we end up isolating and trapping the other person. It is fairly common knowledge that sustaining a long-term relationship takes a lot of work. There are inevitable conflicts and sieges, many of which are beyond our control. But Sting believes that true love means freedom also, and in this regard, "Fortress around Your Heart" forms a nice book-ended companion piece to "If You Love Somebody Set Them Free." In fact, freedom and captivity seem to be the overarching themes of this first solo album. All of the songs, even the instrumental (in my interpretation) deal with one of the other, or both, as a thematic element or undercurrent.

"Fortress around Your Heart" alternates between the keys of g minor and G major, with the chorus situated in the major mode (for the most part). The verses fittingly traverse some pretty rocky terrain harmonically with a couple of surprising chord changes. These distantly related chords (g minor, E♭ dominant 7, and f♯ minor 7) consistently seem fresh both within the repetitions in the song itself and with repeated listenings. It is notable that every time the verse arrives at the idea of "returning," the music seems to get darker as it lands on the f♯ minor 7. This is also, of course, the preparation (musically and allegorically) for building the bridge, reaching the fortress, and setting the heart free in the chorus.

This song could be heard as the most "Police-like" song on the album. The similarities to Police songs are likely due to the Summers-like, minimalist guitar part (here played by Sting) and the Copeland-like drum grooves, alternating between a cool Latin-jazz inspired pattern and a straight-ahead rock chorus (featuring Copeland's signature ride cymbal hits on every beat). It is interesting that the most "conservative" song on the album is closest in style to The Police of the *Synchronicity* period. This speaks to the overall forward-looking aesthetic of *The Dream of the Blue Turtles*.

So to try to answer the questions posed at the beginning of this chapter: Is it really a "solo" album? Is it really a "jazz" album? I think to answer the first, one would have to define further the word "solo." It is a useful term to distinguish a singer's body of work as separate from that produced within a group setting (i.e., to distinguish Paul Simon's solo albums from those with Art Garfunkel). But aside from a very few albums (Paul McCartney comes to mind), in which the artist makes a point of creating all the songs and sounds on an album, "solo" albums are still very much group efforts. The main difference between a group and a solo project is the amount of creative control the songwriter has. Sting had increasingly wanted more of this during The Police years, and this was a factor in the break-up of the band. With *The Dream of the Blue Turtles* he gained creative control, took a great risk, and succeeded.

As far as the "jazz" element, it is mostly a matter of perception. Jazz musicians are naturally more adept at playing a multitude of popular styles. Sting wants this stylistic looseness in any musician playing and working with him, and in his future projects he demanded the same flexibility. The fact that the four musicians that formed his original backing band were African American feels in hindsight more like a coincidence than anything else. In later years, he has worked with people of all different colors and of both genders. He is interested in these people as musicians and colleagues, not as collectibles.

Critical reception to *The Dream of the Blue Turtles* was mixed. Most people admired Sting's boldness in embarking on his solo career in this way, but some were less than impressed by the results of working with these top-grade musicians. The predictable accusations of "selling out" were bandied about, both against Sting (for writing in this new style) and against the band (for working with a charismatic rock star and achieving commercial success). For their peers in the jazz community, the use of the term "sellout" may have indicated simple jealousy at the success of the band known as The Blue Turtles.

Marsalis, in particular, endured the majority of criticism for joining Sting's band from his younger brother Wynton. These two have famously had an on-and-off relationship for most of their adult lives. Wynton, a leader in the traditional jazz movement of the 1980s and 90s, was highly skeptical of Branford's decision to join Sting and even recruit for him. The relationship between Darryl Jones and his former boss Miles Davis was never repaired.

Despite all this behind-the-scenes extramusical drama, *The Dream of the Blue Turtles* is a milestone album in Sting's career and in pop music. The band's chemistry and musical interplay is infectious; one listen to "Shadows in the Rain" and you can't help but smile. The end result of Sting's first solo outing is a fitting launching pad for his later career's stylistically varied jazz-influenced sound, his sophisticated songwriting, and the ambitious and serious content of his lyrics.

BRING ON THE NIGHT

In the fall of 1985, a Sting-commissioned film called *Bring on the Night* was released in theaters. Directed by Michael Apted, it is sort of a documentary but seems to be mostly a concert film. The "documentary" parts of it (interviews with Sting and the band, with Trudie Styler, with Miles Copeland, and others) seem rehearsed and heavily edited for content. Nonetheless, there are a few revealing moments and interesting footage of the band rehearsing for their first public performances since the Ritz shows: playing the Théâtre Mogador in Paris in May 1985. The rehearsals were filmed at Château de Courson outside of Paris.

At some points in the film, one cringes a bit at the obviously staged aspect of some of the situations: the elderly tour group making their way through the room while the band is playing, the "working out" of backing vocal parts with Dolette McDonald and Janice Pendarvis, even though they had recently finished recording the album. But moments like these are forgiven after seeing the exuberant concert footage, which is of course live and is a great display of these talented musicians.

An actual bit of dramatic tension involved the pregnancy and birth of Sting and Styler's second child together, Jake. Styler gave birth to him on the second night of the Mogador shows. Apted (or Sting) decided to allow the cameras into the delivery room, while the soundtrack played "Russians." ("I hope the Russians love their children too.") Poignant, sappy, or tasteless? The critics were divided.

Though the film went on to win a Grammy for best documentary, more artistically successful was the companion live double-CD set, also called *Bring on the Night*. This excellent survey of the Blue Turtles Band's repertoire wasn't released until the following summer, and it includes recordings of shows from both the filmed Mogador shows and the subsequent European tour. On it, Sting includes a mixture of new songs from *The Dream of the Blue Turtles* and older Police material. Since the new songs are largely unchanged from the studio album (although lengthened to allow room for extended solos by Marsalis and Kirkland), I will concentrate my discussion on Sting's reworking of his own songs. Similarly to the new version of "Shadows in the Rain," the re-workings of older material provide a revealing glimpse into Sting's new aesthetic as a solo artist.

The title track is a good example of this. The guitar arpeggios (broken chords) of the original verse are retained (here played with great facility by Sting himself), but the chorus has been "cleaned up" harmonically. In the original (from *Reggatta de Blanc*) one gets the sense that both Sting and Summers weren't quite sure what to make of the chorus. The very last chord that Summers plays, an A (on the word "daylight"), does not jibe harmonically with Sting's bass note of D. Perhaps this was intentional to illustrate the confused state of mind of the speaker, but I doubt it. Sting is reported to have said that he had always hated the chorus.[20]

In the new version of the chorus, that moment gets harmonically clarified, fittingly, with Sting's note of D, this time with the rest of the band harmonizing with him. In addition, the chord on the word "night" has been changed from a somewhat awkward A major chord (in the context of G major, the key of the chorus) to a b minor 7. This leads more smoothly to the following chord (C) and propels the phrase more effectively to the final chords in the pattern: a minor and D. So the entire progression of the chorus is: G-bm7-C-a-D. The register of the lead vocal has also been lowered in the new version. In the original 1979 track, Sting's voice was double-tracked at the octave for the entire song. This had the result of sounding a bit monotonous from an "orchestrational" or tone color standpoint, there being no contrast vocally between the verse and chorus. In the new version, there is a great deal of contrast between these two sections: Sting sings the verses alone and the chorus with Dolette McDonald, Janice Pendarvis, and possibly Omar Hakim.

The revision of "Bring on the Night" is very telling about how far Sting had progressed as a songwriter between 1979 and 1985. The words of the chorus express longing for the night to come (the reason is unspecified), which implies that the verses are happening in the "present" of the speaker's voice. The lessons that Sting learned about "future-focused" choruses seem to come to fruition here. The general malaise of the verses ("The future is but a question mark/Hangs above my head, there in the dark") is eloquently expressed in the "circular" arpeggiated guitar part. But now the chorus seems more relaxed, expressing hope in the coming night. It is a fitting title to both the film and the live album: "Night" implies the touring musician's term for "concert," as in "We played five nights in Germany." For someone like Sting, who enjoys performing and touring, "Night" is when he comes alive.

This track is one of three on the album that are medleys of pairs of songs. It was Branford Marsalis's idea to combine "Bring on the Night" with "When the World Is Running Down."[21] The verse of the first shares a chord pattern and key with the second. On this track, Sting sings the song using the same structure as the original (from *Zenyatta Mondatta*) but then lets the band loose on solos of various kinds. First, a marvelously creative and energetic keyboard solo by Kirkland, and then a playful rap by Marsalis. In 1986, rap was still in its infancy by today's standards and was not a major presence on the charts yet. Therefore, while Marsalis's rap was a novelty for its time, it sounds dated today.

Another exciting medley of songs that works well is "One World (Not Three)/Love Is the Seventh Wave." Both old and new songs share the key of G major (originally) and a medium reggae beat. After an a capella opening chorus from the coda of the original song (on *Ghost in the Machine*), the band kicks in to the song proper. Significantly, this includes a "skank" rhythm in Kirkland's keyboard, the same marimba patch that he used on "Love Is the Seventh Wave." This subtle detail makes the transition to the new song more seamless and helps to clarify the organized unity of the track.

Both of these songs are not harmonically complicated: They are essentially three chords over the bass line centered on G. It is perhaps for this reason that Sting decided to change the key of "Love Is the Seventh Wave" to C major. In what turns out to be the second section in a grand three-part form, he uses this new key to provide harmonic contrast to the rather repetitive G major groove of "One World."

At the end of "Love," Marsalis plays an extended sax solo, and Sting has an impressive guitar solo in the key of a minor. This key may have been chosen for practical reasons: It is relatively easy to solo in, and, Sting not being primarily a guitarist, it may have been more comfortable for him. Nevertheless, a minor does lead quite naturally into A major, with the help of Kirkland's repeated keyboard pattern, which is the key of the return of the "One World" chorus:

Section		Key
A	One World	G
B	Love Is the Seventh Wave	C
	(guitar solo)	a
A'	One World (chorus)	A

As is illustrated in the above diagram, the return of the "One World" material is at a step up in pitch, from G to A. In many songs, this key change simply happens directly, with no pause or music in between. Countless pop songs do this, normally towards the end of the song, to attempt to raise the emotional level during the repetition of the chorus. This technique is called modulation.[22] Sting, in several songs from his solo career, wants to have the same effect but not be so obvious about the key change. He does this by using an intermediary chord that effortlessly arrives at the new pitch level.[23] In this case, he uses C (closely related to the original G), "darkening" it to a minor (for the guitar solo) and then simply "brightening" the key to A major for the return of "One World."

Sting thus makes a quasi-classical three-part or "ABA" form out of this medley of two songs. It is further proof of the malleability of his own material: Many songs lend themselves well to expansion and solo sections. And he is not afraid to rework a song according to the venue or situation. Although he would not release another "official" live album until 2001's . . . *All This Time,* there are many recordings (available as imports or B-sides) that display his range as a skillful arranger of his own catalogue.

Mother and Father

. . . *Nothing Like the Sun*

Sting's second solo studio album, . . . *Nothing Like the Sun,* was released in October 1987. On the whole, it feels more like a typical "solo album," in that the supporting musicians are for the most part different on every song; very unlike *The Dream of the Blue Turtles,* where the core band remained the same. Some key figures from the first band make a reappearance: Marsalis and Kirkland most prominently, but also vocalists Dolette McDonald and Janice Pendarvis, who were both integral parts of the band during the previous tour, film, and live album. For this album, Sting switches back to bass, which gives room to highlight several guest guitarists, most notably Andy Summers. Sting remains primarily on bass for subsequent solo albums.

Generally, . . . *Nothing Like the Sun* feels a bit more coherent than the first album. This is in part due to a common theme that many of the songs share: the mother-son relationship. During the writing of these songs, Sting's mother was dying of cancer; she died while he was recording the album on Montserrat. Women feature prominently in many songs; in the periodical *Timeout,* Sting observes: "I look back on this album and I realize that the record is about my mother, although I didn't see it at the time. It's about mothers and daughters, mistresses and wives, sisters . . . It's all about women."[1]

The album title is another Shakespeare quote, this time from the opening of sonnet 130: "My mistress's eyes are nothing like the sun." This poem is about the author's perception of his love as imperfect, but ends with the couplet "And yet, by heaven, I think my love as rare / as any she belied with false compare." So, in the end, it is not one of the bitter poems, but rather a sweet love poem and meditation on the beauty of imperfection. Sting also isolates this line as the title of his album (even though he uses the full-line quotation in the track "Sister Moon") in order to emphasize the pun on the word "sun/son." Sting was very close to his mother as a boy, and they stayed in touch throughout his professional life and during his parents' divorce and remarriage.

The album sold well, despite its initial release as a two-record set in the LP version. The year 1987 was still a transitional time for the music industry, and artists were releasing albums in three formats: LP, cassette, and CD. . . . *Nothing Like the Sun* peaked at No. 9 on the Billboard chart, thanks to its only truly successful single (by Sting's standards), "We'll Be Together," which reached No. 7. Other singles did not fare as well: "Englishman in New York," "Fragile," and "They Dance Alone" did not chart. "Be Still My Beating Heart" charted at No. 15. Given the generally somber mood of the album, this is not surprising. There are wonderful songs on this album, but most would not be considered "radio-friendly" from a Top-40 radio format perspective. Indeed, "We'll Be Together" was retooled, rerecorded, and generally "funked up" after the original version was deemed not sufficient to fulfill the important slot of first single; A&M Records brought in producer Bryan Loren to help Sting rework this song. The first version of this song can be heard on the greatest hits collection *Fields of Gold,* released in 1994.

The album starts off with a fittingly exuberant elegy to his mother: "The Lazarus Heart." This is one of those Sting songs that in my opinion are his best: those that have a deep and rather dark (but thematically rich) lyric, but with a pop-savvy exuberance that one can dance to. The song is in C, but it uses the mixolydian scale, which is a major scale with a lowered seventh. This scale is frequently used in jazz and popular and folk music, and it has a quality that may be described as "happy, but relaxed." The main tune of the verse sounds quite folk song-like. In "The Lazarus Heart" there are also occasional flashes of dissonance (in the synthesizer and in Andy Summers's guitar) that seem to me to be bright glints in this sonic landscape of polished bronze. The vaguely West African groove is supplied by French drummer Manu Katché, who had previously played with Peter Gabriel and has since become one of the industry's most sought after studio drummers. The African influence is not surprising, given the year the album was recorded: a year after the phenomenal success of Paul Simon's *Graceland.*

Structurally, the song does not do much of note: After an introduction, verse and chorus alternate, with a soprano sax solo after the second chorus and more solos during the fade at the end. However, right before the third verse at the end of Marsalis's solo, the band speeds up the groove by 75 percent so that they squeeze four measures into the space of three. This kind of rhythmic play (called "metric modulation") is common in postwar jazz and serves the function of momentary disorientation, purely in the spirit of fun.

Sting mentions in the liner notes to the album and in many subsequent interviews that this lyric grew out of a dream he had. Like the dream of the blue turtles destroying his garden, he interpreted it as being of great importance and created a piece of music out of it. In this case, his dream involved a real person from his life: his mother. She has "cut him open," giving him a wound that gives him "courage and pain." This wound most probably represents her death, which we know affected him deeply: "It was a real nightmare about my mother's death because I was feeling totally powerless."[2] The "lovely flower" that grows from the wound is, quite possibly, the album that follows. In this light, "The Lazarus Heart" is a perfect opener for this album that explores various aspects of the mother-son relationship.

Lazarus is the man Jesus raises from the dead in the New Testament miracle story. In this song, Sting is wishing that he could be the blood of this man's heart, coursing through his resurrected body. Blood is a common image through the whole song, not just in the chorus: Sting mentions the "wound" in the first and second verses; in the third verse he mentions his mother counting her children as a shield against the pain. Indirectly, this verse refers to the blood, courage, and pain of childbirth.

Moreover, by this time Sting had four children of his own. He could now count them as a shield against his own pain. Are the birds on his mother's house in the third verse possibly symbols for children? Or are they symbols of death, who will eventually visit him? It almost goes without saying that this is deep subject matter, yet each individual image in the song has its own internal logic, much like the surreal logic of a dream.

The next song shares the word "heart" in its title but could not be more different. "Be Still My Beating Heart" is about *eros,* or the sexual form of love. In some situations it can be called lust. The situation that Sting describes is left unclear so that he can focus on the physical and psychological effects of *eros.* One of the first things to go by the wayside is logic, so the speaker's search for knowledge about lust is fruitless. His "logic has drowned in a sea of emotion," like the stone that sinks in the previous line of the chorus. The use of ocean and water imagery is fitting, as in Jungian terms water represents the unconscious, irrational mind.

The music that accompanies this lyric about self-restraint and inaction has a wonderful sense of "bubbling under the surface." The bass part is a crucial element in this representation of contained energy. Sting plays two basic patterns; one each for the verse and the chorus. They both seem to belong to a faster song, as though the groove established by Katché is the representation of self-restraint. During the faded-in introduction (implying a continuous state), Sting plays the chorus bass riff. The change to the new riff signals the coming of the verse.

The few times when the music seems to relax are during the chorus (when the speaker attempts to calm himself using logic and reason) and during the middle eight (where the speaker comments on the futility of perfection). In each of these spots, the animated bass-line is absent, which implies that the bass represents the "beating heart" of the title. Also, as we have seen in previous Sting songs, the middle eight is used as an attempted escape from the song's situation. Here, he uses the brighter relative major key, C, to illustrate the idea of futility, as mentioned above. This section slips effortlessly back into the second half of the chorus: "I sink like a stone that's been thrown in the ocean." We leave the song with a still-restrained but almost bursting coda that features Andy Summers and Kirkland soloing over a double-time beat by Katché. The fade-out implies continuation, and here the implication is that this sexual tension will ultimately boil over.

The mood is lightened considerably by the next song, "Englishman in New York." Even though it is in a minor key, Sting's buoyant melody and snappy rhythm capture the quiet and crisp elegance of the subject: Sting's fellow Englishman in New York, Quentin Crisp (1908–1999). By this time Sting had purchased an apartment in Manhattan and had written most of these songs there.[3] Crisp was an openly gay, eccentric author and actor with a wicked sense of humor and fun, as can be seen in Jonathan Nossiter's documentary about Crisp's life as a homosexual British expatriate, *Resident Alien*. Sting was interviewed for the documentary and appears in a few snippets. Sting and Crisp met while working on *The Bride,* a Franc Roddam–directed adaptation of the Frankenstein story. The movie bombed and was deservedly torn apart by the critics. Crisp had just a bit part, despite his much greater acting experience than Sting—one of his most memorable roles was as Queen Elizabeth I in Sally Potter's *Orlando* (1992). The two men hit it off and met several times while Sting was in New York.

"Englishman in New York" is a song that seems to deliberately confuse the speaker with the author. On the surface, if a listener knew nothing about the origins of the song, she might think it was purely autobiographical. However, Sting's explanation that it's about Quentin Crisp seems to settle the matter. But, over the course of the song, the line "Be yourself, no matter what they say" emerges as the main message. It first appears at the end of verse three, returns on the reprise of that verse (after verse four), and then is repeated underneath the coda's repetition of the chorus during the fade-out. Sting has increasingly needed to remember to be himself over the years, having endured mountains of criticism (mainly from the mainstream rock press) for changing styles upon going solo, not to mention the break-up of both The Police and his first marriage. So, the speaker of this song and its author are conflated, but in the end it is Sting's voice that comes through.

Sting takes the adage "Manners maketh man," coined by William of Wykeham (1324–1404)[4] and teases more layers out of this expression. Sting probably heard it during childhood at the dinner table and at St. Cuthbert's Grammar School, exhorting young people to use etiquette to distinguish themselves from animals. ("Don't eat like a pig," would be the American equivalent.) But in this song, Sting narrows the scope of it to the male sex and uses it as a springboard to explore the idea of masculinity.

But Sting refers to a kind of contemporary masculinity that is in some ways a throwback to Victorian England's values. For many, the ideal contemporary man is not necessarily marked by physical strength or many of the other traditional masculine virtues, the kind referred to in verse four as "combat gear" and guns. Masculinity today is a complex set of qualities, many of which in other times might have seen as feminine, and also which in the late twentieth century became even more complex with the more public addition of homosexuality to the mix. A full exploration of this topic is beyond the scope of this book, but this song does ultimately ask the question, "What is a man?"

Seen in this light, one can hear the song's opening groove as a wonderful combination of "masculine" and "feminine" symbols. Since this is a "layered" rhythm (with off-beat eighth notes in the synthesized string part, the bass on every quarter note, and the bass drum on every other quarter; i.e., twice as slow), it feels like a reggae-derived rhythm. But the use of a *pizzicato* (plucked) string sound in Kirkland's keyboard gives it a light bounce and, in my opinion, a certain feminine quality. I think that Sting was trying to capture the essence of Quentin Crisp musically; walking down the street with a calm, slightly odd, and effeminate ease, and of course a "civilized" walking cane.

The song's structure is fairly typical: alternating verse-chorus, with a middle eight that begins in the brighter relative major key of D (the main key of the song is b minor). This middle section winds up, however, after a sequence of classically inspired chords, back at b minor. Then, a complete change of style and groove (although still using the same chords as the verse) into a bebop-style Marsalis solo, accompanied by the rhythm section of Sting, Kirkland, and Katché. After four times through the "changes" (the jazz term for chord progression), we hear yet another huge stylistic shift into that of a rap or hip-hop drum pattern. And then, just as suddenly, we enter back into the cultured world of refinement and etiquette for verse four. After the coda of the repeated chorus, simultaneously with the "moral" of the song (mentioned above), Marsalis's lonely sax solo fades away like a solitary musician on a balcony somewhere in Greenwich Village.

Sting has said that for the middle of this song, he wanted to create the effect of looking into doors of nightclubs as the listener is walking down the street.[5] This is quite effective in portraying Crisp (as well as the listeners) as an "outsider" looking in at various musical styles, as well as in providing a brief snapshot of the popular music scene of New York at the time. On another level, though (and connecting to the theme of the lyrics), it can be heard as observing various expressions of masculinity: the "cool" bebop style first and the heavy rap beat second. Both of these styles can safely be labeled primarily "masculine" in nature (especially in the male-dominated world of 1987 rap). Ultimately, the moral of "be yourself" shines through musically with Marsalis's lonely solo during the fade-out. This also expresses a third traditional quality of masculinity: the occasional and necessary desire for solitude.

The next song, "History Will Teach Us Nothing," is a good example of Sting's cynical side. He mentions in the liner notes that he was disillusioned by the subject of history in school. It's easy to see how: A browse through any history book does in fact seem like a "monotonous and sordid succession of robber baron scumbags."[6] This view of history can certainly challenge any optimist.

Sting does, in fact, end the song on a note of hope, but along the way he focuses on successions of power struggles with the common features of war and fear. Each verse in turn discusses freedom, religion, power, and war. The chorus of "sooner or later" is rather opaque (except generally addressing the subject of time) until just after the fourth verse. At this point we hear the title of the song for the first time (despite the incorrect printing in the CD booklet, only partially corrected in 2007's *Lyrics by Sting*), and then a change of key from a minor to A major. With the brightening of the key, we hear the more hopeful completion of the fragment "sooner or later." There is a hint of Jamaican patois in the line "Just like the world first day," with its dropped possessive. Also, Sting channels Bob Marley on the line from verse two "Without the voice of reason." As in earlier Police songs, I believe this is not mockery, but homage.

The song does not remain in the happier key of A major but keeps returning to the minor sound as if to remind us that history keeps repeating itself. Even during the coda, after an assertion of the power of human rights, the music returns to a minor, following a final "sooner or later." So this is optimism tempered by realism.

Although not one of his strongest lyrics, the reggae groove is one of the best on the album. Katché's hits during the choruses are very effective, as everything else he plays is quite subdued. Percussionist Mino Cinelu also plays an important role in this track. Sting plays electric guitar in addition to bass on this song, and he obviously had fun with the "wah-wah" pedal (a foot-controlled device that squelches or opens up the overtones of the sound, depending on how far back or forward one's heel is). Marsalis contributes a mournful soprano sax refrain, first heard in the introduction and later combined with the title words.

"History Will Teach Us Nothing" is one of a handful of songs in Sting's catalogue that seems to have been changed in the latter stages of recording and production. The printed lyrics in both the CD and LP versions do not exactly match what is sung on the recording.[7] In this case, the difference is slight, but significant: The first chorus is sung as "sooner or later," still in the minor key that we started with. In the CD booklet, the longer, later version of the chorus (in the major mode) is printed at this point in the song. It is my belief that Sting changed his mind about the placement of the chorus, and thus also the change of key, after the lyric sheet was laid out and sent to the printer. Either that or it was simply an oversight. The final version makes for a much more effective structure; saving the major key for later on in the song and also reducing the overall number of key changes.

Changing gears somewhat, the next track, "They Dance Alone," seems to be a response to the question posed by the previous song: Are we doomed to repeat history? In the case of South America, the unfortunate answer seems to be yes. The continent struggled throughout the twentieth century to break the cycle of corruption, chaos, and dictatorship, with a few success stories and signs of hope. Yet it still seems that these countries have one foot planted in the Third World.

One country that is far better off now than in 1987 is Chile. Augusto Pinochet's CIA-backed military junta wrested power from the legitimately elected Allende government in 1973. Their practice of "disappearing" people (arresting, imprisoning, torturing, and executing political opponents and innocent people without trial) was still being used as late as 1986, when Sting toured the world and visited Chile as part of Amnesty International's "Conspiracy of Hope" tour. Pinochet's regime was finally toppled in 1990, and he died peacefully in exile in 2006, despite several attempts to convict him of crimes against humanity.

This regime not only suppressed any and all political opposition, but also every art form and artist that was deemed dangerous or offensive in any way. This included the playing of traditional Chilean and Andean folk music.[8] The *cueca*[9] is one of the most popular folk-dance songs in the country and was outlawed in 1973. However, Sting learned firsthand during his 1986 tour that mothers, wives, and daughters of these "disappeared" men would dance this dance, silently, with giant photographs of their loved ones hanging from their necks. This brave act was simultaneously protest, mourning, and an expression of love.[10]

The faded-in introduction sets the stage: The ominous "military"-style snare drum flourishes, countered by the synthesized pan flute (a traditional Andean instrument), which represents the grieving women, some of whom were indigenous Chileans.[11] The choice of this synthesizer patch is apt, if a bit of a cliché, since all of the traditional Andean music, and by extension, instruments, were banned by the regime. Thus the instrument itself becomes part of the protest.

Sting uses each verse to address an aspect of the scene. In the first, he wonders why these women are dancing alone a dance normally done with a partner. In the second, the focus is on their enforced silence: If they speak out they could be arrested. The third verse is directed at the man responsible for this situation, Pinochet himself. It speaks of this man's tenuous hold on power, based as it is on foreign investment from like-minded regimes. This verse also brings the song full circle thematically, asking Pinochet directly to imagine his own mother performing the *cueca* solo.[12] Once again, Sting is infusing a bleak situation with hope.

The middle section, beginning with "One day we'll dance on their graves" becomes more important after the last chorus. Here, in a moment of exhilarating musical transformation, the same chord progression is used to create a *samba,* another South American dance, but one of pure joy. The beat gets doubled exactly, but the chord changes do not speed up, and so the transition is smooth and magical. The band lets the groove build, with repeated vocal parts of "And we'll dance," until Marsalis enters with a buoyant soprano saxophone. It is hard to find a better representation of hope for the future in a popular song.

One frustrating element of this track is the mix. Sting has several guests in the studio with him, most audibly actor and musician Ruben Blades, who speaks the words of the chorus in Spanish (over music from the introduction).[13] The other three guests are notable guitarists Fareed Haque, Mark Knopfler, and Eric Clapton (all playing acoustic guitar), who unfortunately are so low in the final mix that they are practically inaudible. They play most audibly during the spoken section, under Blades, but in general don't ultimately contribute much to the sound.

"They Dance Alone" and the following song, "Fragile," are both significant in Sting's output for being some of the first to address human rights and their abuses. The "Conspiracy of Hope" tour, including meeting with victims of torture and the Mothers of the Disappeared, had a profound impact on his output and his career. These two songs are also the most Latin-influenced songs on the album, which led some early reviews to dub . . . *Nothing Like the Sun* his "South American" album. In truth, it is only these two songs, plus possibly "Straight to My Heart," that explicitly use this style.

In any case, "Fragile" is a straightforward minor-key *balada*-style track, featuring Sting on acoustic guitar. The song is framed by an introductory section, which becomes the coda at the end. This introduction alternates two synth chords while Sting plays fragments of the vocal melody on guitar. The main guitar melody, once the rhythm section starts, is a lovely, haunting series of parallel sixths. This interval is typical of Spanish classical guitar music; it is relatively easy to play and yet has melodic and harmonic interest.

This guitar pattern becomes a countermelody to the vocal line, which is deliberately soft and understated. "Too many cooks can spoil the pot," as the saying goes, and so it is true in songwriting also. If you have too many melodies and musical ideas in one song, it can become confusing for the listener. Here Sting wisely opts for simplicity, both in musical material and in the song's structure. Aside from the introduction, there really are only two musical sections: the verse and the chorus. The impressive guitar solo uses the same chordal pattern as the verse. The chorus is very similar to the second half of the verse, using the same last three chords of a minor, B, and e minor. Also the harmonization of the melody in parallel sixths continues. The only difference happens during the last two repetitions of the line "how fragile we are," when Sting descends from e minor down to C and back up. This is a typical move in this style, and he saves it for the end to provide contrast to the following coda.

The framing coda is almost exactly like the introduction, save for the addition of some guitar arpeggios (rapid broken cords) and at the very end, a final cadence on the home chord of e minor. The very last gesture is a quick ascending harp-like arpeggio that ends with a musical question: The passage ends on the F♯, or a dissonant scale degree two in this key of e minor. The energy and direction of this gesture really points towards another note in the pattern, a G, but it is left unfulfilled. This has the psychoacoustic effect of being unfinished, despite the final low e bass note, and thus ends the song with a question mark.

The question seems to be the eternal "why?" Why do people still resort to violence to attempt to solve their problems? Will violence ever stop? Why do people kill? Sting keeps the point of view of the song very general, which is perhaps why it has been taken up by the environmental movement[14] and by people grieving after the 9/11 terrorist attacks. In 2001, during the rehearsals and recording of the live album . . . *All This Time,* Sting fashioned a new version of "Fragile" with expanded instrumentation and harmonies.

As general as the lyric seems, there may be a touch of Sting's voice here. The ultimate message is that violence begets violence and that people "born beneath an angry star" need to exercise restraint in the face of that animalistic fighting instinct. Sting has described himself as full of rage as a young man: "One of the biggest influences the Sex Pistols had on me was that they were destroying something which had held me back . . . I could relate to that anti-establishment feeling. The energy and aggression—hatred!"[15] A revealing scene in Stewart Copeland's 2006 documentary *Everyone Stares: The Police Inside and Out* shows a bit of that rage: In a partially staged sequence, Copeland films Summers "nonchalantly" exploring the train compartment that Sting is sitting in, listening to music through headphones. As Summers gets closer and increasingly annoying, Sting explodes in profanity-laced fury at Summers and tackles him to the floor. The episode soon dissolves into adolescent laughter, but Sting's anger is visceral and almost palpable.

A complete contrast, "We'll Be Together," began the original "side two" of the cassette version of the album and disc two (or "side three") of the original LP pressing. In the LP era, the first song on the second side was crucial: It was a new beginning in the middle of a record, but of course people had the choice of just listening to side one. The song in that spot had to keep people listening and was often therefore an up-tempo, annunciatory type of song.[16]

"We'll Be Together" is very blatantly a dance track, with a heavy, funk-derived beat that was typical for mid-80s pop. Also from funk it borrows a bass effect that simultaneously duplicates the note an octave up (the octave duplicator). This gives the bass note a more biting presence in the mix. Musically, the most notable thing is Sting's voice. Compared to many of his earlier solo tracks, his vocal style seems much looser and more playful on this song. The backing vocalists during the chorus focus on a high D,[17] and Sting in the coda actually surpasses that note to sing an F above it. This is the highest note he has sung on record.

The song's structure is nothing special: a verse-chorus alternation with a middle eight using some contrasting chords. The most interesting thing that happens harmonically is the coda. After a final "break" chorus (with no musical accompaniment, just drums), the chord pattern changes to B♭, g minor-d minor and continues under the backing vocalists' repetition of the song title. In between these repetitions, Sting does another of his self-quotations, this time from the previous album's first single, "If You Love Somebody Set Them Free." In fact, up to now, his pattern was to quote the previous album's hit single in the coda of a song on the new album; a pattern that will be broken on the following album, *The Soul Cages*.

It is quite revealing to compare the single version of "We'll Be Together" with the original version included on the greatest hits compilation *Fields of Gold*. This version is sparer, a tick slower, and includes a prominent electric guitar (played by Eric Clapton). The bass and drums are not as present, there is no coda with the self-quotation, and in general the song sounds rather anemic. Like the rest of the album, this track was produced by Neil Dorfsman. Bryan Loren was brought in to create a more marketable, radio-friendly version.

Although no one would consider "We'll Be Together" subversive, it does bend the rules a bit. Dance music is naturally associated with the body and thus carries connotations and both implicit and explicit sexual messages in the lyrics and overall style. Most dance tracks could generally be classified as "love songs," although of the lusty libidinous kind. This song, while using the musical style associated with sexual love and lust, has lyrics that are purely about *romantic* love. It is about staying together, not philandering, flirting, or physical intimacy. This is why the quote from "If You Love Somebody Set Them Free" is apt. This is a love song for an established couple, celebrating their love on the dance floor.

"Straight to My Heart" is another song that has a vaguely South American flavor, mainly due to Mino Cinelu's percussion. This song is one of the first Sting songs to use an unusual time signature: $7/8$.[18] On later albums he will show a predilection for asymmetrical meters (the number of beats in a measure, which is a basic unit of musical time). The use of these time signatures probably comes from his jazz-rock roots and playing with Last Exit. It actually has very little to do with Latin American music.

But this hybrid creates a great song. The percussion-only introduction deliberately obscures the beat and really only functions to establish the sixteenth note constant. Soon the keyboards and bass introduce the musical "germ" of the song: an elaboration of a b minor chord harmonized with a descending chromatic internal line. The two phrases played twice through make up one verse. After another verse we get a verse/refrain, which begins on a chord a step below and descends to an F♯ before bouncing back up to the tonic of b and the statement of the title words (the refrain).

This pattern of verse and verse/refrain (so named because of the title words appearing at the end of the stanza) repeats and leads to the joyous midsection in the relative major key of D. This section almost functions as a chorus, since the words are identical each time it appears: "Come in to my door/ Be the light of my life." The addition of clapping and a flute sound serve to further lighten the mood. At the end of this middle section, the texture thins, and on the words "I'll be true," Sting sings an ascending stepwise melody that is mirrored in the bass (i.e., stepwise down).

Then, at this halfway point in the song, we go back to the beginning, and the whole structure repeats (with new words, and with the exception of one verse at the beginning of the structure instead of two). This type of musical structure is called binary, meaning "two parts." The song can be divided roughly in half, with the same musical events happening in sequence in each half. After the final "I'll be true," the cycle begins again. This time, however, the opening music becomes the coda of the song, and we fade out in essentially the same way we began, except that here the verse and the refrain are overlaid and repeated. A large part of what makes this song so fun to listen to is the rhythmic interplay between the consistent bass/keyboard pattern and Cinelu's and Katché's percussive additions to the mix.

This is a song where the music outweighs the lyrics in terms of quality. In a songwriter's craft there are generally three methods of working: (1) Write the music first and put some words onto the melody; (2) write the music and words simultaneously; or (3) write the words first (or have someone else write them) and then set them to music. Any of these approaches can be appropriate for any given song. "Straight to My Heart" feels like the first type, where the music came first. The lyrics seem to be about biotechnology creating love in some future time. The speaker is telling his lover that even though "they" may someday invent this technology, his love is true. Although there are several forced rhymes along the way, it is essentially a courting song, with the clearest section being the joyful middle: "Come into my door . . . come and be my wife."

"Rock Steady" is another one of the weaker songs on the album. The title puns on the intermediate style of Jamaican popular music, between ska and reggae. This style had its heyday in the mid-1960s, before the full flowering of reggae in 1969.[19] The title more strongly refers to several elements of the song, as rather than having a rock steady rhythm, this song is in a 12/8 "shuffle," propelled constantly by Sting's upright bass and Katché's playing. It is also a "story song" with no variation in the verse-chorus alternating structure. The end of each verse has a descending chromatic bass-line that ends up on the dominant before returning to the tonic for the chorus.

Sting's version of the Noah and the flood story seems to be updated to the present day, or else Sting is using contemporary language—like "newspaper" and "radio"—to tell his version of this ancient story. Either way, Sting compresses the main elements into three verses, which leaves little room for development or detail. The speaker is an additional character who, accompanied by his girlfriend, signs up to help the Noah figure. They help, and they do get saved from the flood, but they feel trapped and enslaved, so they send a bird to find land (in the original, it is Noah who sends the dove).

The chorus, which happens after every verse, alternately refers to "Noah's" confidence in the ark, the speaker's confidence in "Noah," and the rock that the dove finds at the end of the song. But the musical setting of the words "rock steady" deliberately go against the apparent solidity of the rock. This musical text painting of an unspoken unease with the Noah figure (at least at the beginning) is clever, but the use of the same unstable music for the final chorus does not offer any comfort. So it seems the speakers are in the same place that they began, despite being saved from the flood.

What does make "Rock Steady" fun to listen to is the sonic variety of the track: the interplay between Marsalis and Kirkland, animal sounds, storm sounds, vocalizations of the backing vocalists. For me, these details save the song from dullness. In the hands of a lesser songwriter and producer, a song like this would not make the final cut.

"Sister Moon" was originally the first track on the last side of the two-LP version of . . . *Nothing Like the Sun*, and it has a sort of "homestretch" feel to it. The nocturnal setting seems to fit at this point in the album: a night song after the "rebirth" of the "Lazarus Heart" and daytime songs such as "Englishman in New York" and "Fragile." This view of the order of songs following the arc of the day is perhaps tenuous, but track order is in many cases an agonizing decision process, and this may have served as a loose template on which to place the songs. Moreover, song order can greatly affect how listeners perceive and remember an album.[20]

Sting says in the liner notes that "Sister Moon" is "a song for lunatics everywhere," and he is possibly including himself in that category. The song contains the kernel of this album: his love for his recently deceased mother and his explanation of why he has chosen the path that he has. In relation to the album as a whole it points to a strong thematic connection to the mother figure. Despite the title's reference to the moon as a sister, the women in this song are also mother (verse two) and mistress (verse three). This implies that Sting is singing about the eternal feminine, a Jungian concept with which he is undoubtedly familiar; an individual woman, after all, can be all three at once (mother of children, sister, and lover).

In verse three, Sting's choice of album title becomes clear. "My mistress's eyes are nothing like the sun" is the first line of Shakespeare's sonnet 130, which lists how the lover's qualities do not measure up to this or that, but ends with the couplet "And yet I think my love as rare / As any she belied with false compare." In other words, the poet's love is unique, special, and cannot be described through conventional comparisons.

Sting's use of this line is telling, because it speaks to the idea of "false compare"—comparison of people to some idea of perfection (also referred to in "Consider Me Gone"). Sting's "comparison" here, on the surface, is of the moon and the sun; but it works on a deeper level of comparing the mother with the son (along with the pun on "sun"). Typically, in many mythologies, the sun is seen as masculine and the moon as feminine. Sting's next line, forming a couplet with the Shakespeare line, relates his career as a musician, songwriter, and performer to his "hunger" for the feminine. The "howling" of the next line could be a reference to his singing career as well as an image of a lunatic, and the last statement of the refrain ("I'd go out of my mind but for you") makes more sense in relation to a female figure serving as an anchor for his life and emotional state.

The music of "Sister Moon" heightens the connections among the many levels of the song. The nocturnal mood is ushered in by the solo soprano saxophone, in one of Marsalis's best contributions to the album. Kirkland's synthesized strings are full of lush, Gershwinesque harmonies that swell and fade over Sting's upright bass. The atmosphere is masterfully created before the first note is sung. The two opening chords ($f\sharp m\sharp^{79}$ and B^{79}) serve as an "anchor" for the whole song in that they underscore the first part of the verse and return on the refrain.

The most interesting section of the song happens at the beginning of verse three (which initially feels like the middle eight; in retrospect we realize that it is an altered verse), on the crucial line from Shakespeare. The key changes up a third, and Sting's vocal line is therefore higher than the rest of the song. The third line of this verse effects the change back into the original key (of $f\sharp$ minor), and it is done so smoothly that we don't even realize that it is happening. During the last refrain, Sting sings the line "And they really don't care if I do" instead of the established refrain. On the word "do" there is what is called a "deceptive cadence" (from classical terminology): The chord pattern, instead of moving V–I like a typical cadence, does V–VI, thus "deceiving" the listener into expecting the phrase to end on the home chord of I (but it doesn't). Here, the final cadence does not happen until the last note of the refrain, thus re-establishing the home key and returning to the $F\sharp$-B anchor of the opening. Thus, the metaphoric connection between the home key, the moon, the eternal feminine, and Sting's career and emotional life are crystallized in this one moment. Heard this way, it is hard to imagine a more personal and emotionally powerful song in his catalogue.

Another "personal" song, even though it is not an original, is the next track, Jimi Hendrix's "Little Wing." Since this book focuses on Sting as a songwriter, I will not discuss the music of this song per se but will instead talk about the reasons for its inclusion on the album. Among Sting's solo albums, it is the only cover that he has done, and therefore it must be regarded as an important song to him.

The path that this song took to make it onto . . . *Nothing Like the Sun* is a circuitous one. Sting heard the Jimi Hendrix Experience live as a 16-year-old in 1967 in Newcastle. It was a transformative experience for him:

> The Jimi Hendrix Experience was an overwhelming, deafening wave of sound that simply obliterated analysis. I think I remember snatches of "Hey Joe" and

"Foxy Lady," but that event remains a blur of noise and breathtaking virtuosity, of Afro'd hair, wild clothes, and towers of Marshall amplifiers. It was also the first time I'd ever seen a black man . . . I lay in my bed that night with my ears ringing and my worldview significantly altered.[21]

Almost 20 years later, Sting introduced himself to Gil Evans, one of the twentieth-century's greatest big band leaders and arrangers. Evans (1912–1988) had previously done an entire album of Jimi Hendrix arrangements (1974's *The Gil Evans Orchestra Plays the Music of Jimi Hendrix*).[22] Evans invited Sting to sing with his band, which eventually led to an evening-length concert at the 1987 Umbria Jazz Festival in Perugia, Italy. This concert recording is only available as a bootleg; the track listing tells us that, in addition to Hendrix covers and standards, they did a few Police and Sting songs as well, arranged for big band by Evans and his assistant, Maria Schneider.[23]

One of the songs they did together was "Little Wing." The original studio version appears on Hendrix's 1967 album *Axis: Bold as Love*. Evans had arranged it for his 1974 album and again for his 1985 *Farewell* album,[24] and he expanded the original song's structure to include space for soloists. Indeed, the original Hendrix studio version is only two and a half minutes long. Evans (and Sting) gives the song more shape by essentially playing the song twice, with a guitar solo in the middle. The guitar player on . . . *Nothing Like the Sun* version was Hiram Bullock, at that time a young rising star of the jazz-funk scene. Bullock certainly delivers a fiery performance, with a conscious homage to Hendrix's original solo during the final fade-out.

A confusing credit in the booklet of this album state that "Gil Evans and his orchestra play on this track." But if one listens closely, one is hard-pressed to hear any big band at all. The music seems to be all created by Kirkland's synthesizers. Since this album was exclusively recorded at Air Studios in Montserrat (no other recording locations are mentioned), it would have been too expensive to hire and transport an entire big band to record just one song. My contention is that Sting used Evans's arrangement of the song (the 1985 version, which Bullock and Egan had recorded with Evans), and Kirkland emulated the sound of a big band with his keyboards. The "orchestra" credited is really just Hiram Bullock, Mark Egan on bass, and Kenwood Dennard on drums. Bullock and Egan had played with Evans's band for a few years and had performed this song several times, and Dennard is a much sought after studio drummer.

What is most important for our purposes is the meaning of the song. The fantastic and psychedelic-influenced lyrics could either suggest a drug-induced seduction or a supernatural communication. The most significant lines for the latter interpretation is "When I'm sad she comes to me / with a thousand smiles she gives to me free." In this way, "Little Wing" has a similar sentiment as "Sister Moon": Connection or communication with a female muse will help him get through this time of sorrow and depression. And he will channel that grief into music making.

As "Little Wing" fits nicely into . . . *Nothing Like the Sun*'s theme of the spectrum of female figures, so does the final song, "The Secret Marriage." As Sting states in the liner notes, the melody was adapted from a song by German expatriate composer Hanns Eisler (1898–1962). "An dem kleinem Radio-apparat" ("To the Little Radio") was one of the collaborations between Eisler and Bertolt Brecht, who together created several communist musical-theater pieces in the 1930s.[25] This particular song is from the collection called *Die Hollywood-Elegien* (*Hollywood Elegies*), published in 1942, while Eisler and Brecht were both living in Hollywood. The subject of the original poem is living in exile, and it is a bittersweet ode to a radio brought from the old country. The sentiment is "please don't fall silent, little radio, even if I have to still hear from my enemies and about everything I've lost."

Sting chose to expand this short song, similarly to "Little Wing." Instead of the one and a half verses of the original, Sting creates three verses plus a chorus by repeating and expanding the music.

Eisler	Sting
A	A (verse 1)
A'	A (verse 2)
B	B (chorus)
	A' (verse 3)
	B (chorus)

Although Sting's words have nothing to do with living in exile, they do retain the longing beauty of the original mood and suit his purposes well.

Sting says that this song is for Trudie Styler, who at the time was still unmarried (they married in 1992). "We expressed our vows to each other every day, but not in a big public ceremony."[26] This album progresses from the opening song about a mother (the first woman a child knows), to a song about marriage (the embodiment of the Jungian concept of *anima*). It is a wonderful ending to one of the strongest albums in Sting's catalogue.

THE SOUL CAGES

Sting spent the next three years touring, fundraising for various social causes (including the Rainforest Foundation, an organization started by himself and Styler to protect the rights of indigenous people in the Amazon), acting (in *Julia and Julia* opposite Kathleen Turner and in Mike Figgis's *Stormy Monday*), and buying property all around the world. Christopher Sandford postulates that he was keeping himself occupied so as not to grieve his parents' deaths (his father died in 1989). He did, in fact, suffer writer's block, although for a mercifully brief time (only about two years), and the fallow period resulted in what some regard as one of his best albums, *The Soul Cages*, released in 1991.

The overall tone of this album is quite dark, from the bleak view of the working class in "Island of Souls" to the atheistic hopelessness of "Why Should I Cry for You?" to the minor key instrumental "Saint Agnes and the Burning Train." Even the album art is abstract and moody,[27] featuring only two pictures of Sting, a record low. There are no chatty liner notes either, as there were in the previous two albums. Still, Sting has stood by this album as a necessary step and a natural part of his grieving process: "I couldn't get away from these ideas about my background, my father, death. I had to get them out of the way, almost as part of the mourning process, so I could then get on with writing songs for fun."[28]

On *The Soul Cages,* Sting goes back to a core "band" idea that plays on almost every song. This band includes guitarist Dominic Miller for the first time, who has since collaborated with Sting on every album. Kenny Kirkland returns, as do Manu Katché and Branford Marsalis, although Marsalis plays a more limited role than on the previous albums. Sting does all the vocals and so did not need the services of McDonald and Pendarvis. For the subsequent tour, Katché was replaced by drummer Vinnie Colaiuta, who has also since become a regular member of the band. This album went to No. 1 on the British charts and reached No. 2 on the Billboard album chart.

The damp northern mood of the first track, "Island of Souls," is immediately set by Kathryn Tickell's Northumbrian pipes, playing a modal tune reminiscent of northern English folk song. Northumbrian pipes (also known as "small pipes") are similar to typical Scottish bagpipes except that they are operated by using a bellows instead of blowing. Soon Kirkland's keyboards and Katché's cymbals and light percussion establish an ocean-like groove with occasional flashes of the riveters' guns. The first time I heard this song, I was unsure where to feel the beat. Especially when Sting begins the mostly stepwise melody of the opening verse, the meter is deliberately confused. This song is in a hybrid meter of 6/8 and 3/4, with the keyboards and drums usually expressing the 6/8 (two beats per measure) and the voice and bass expressing 3/4 (three beats per measure). Since both of these measures have the same number of eighth notes (six), they take the same amount of time. The eighth notes are grouped into either groups of two or three. This idea permeates the song and gives it a fascinating rhythmic texture.

"Island of Souls" tells the story, in a set of succinctly drawn vignettes, of "Billy," the son of a shipbuilder, and how his father dies in an "industrial accident." This story has been repeated all too often among the working classes; men who work all their lives and then die because of the industry. For Sting, the ships that would get taller and taller next to his childhood home symbolized death.[29] The irony is that these workers spend all their working lives building their own "death."

The previously mentioned stepwise (or mostly stepwise) verse melody is based on the same folk-influenced scale used in "We Work the Black Seam" (Dorian). Sting allows himself plenty of melodic freedom in the following verses—the melodies themselves are different, but they essentially retain the same shape and general stepwise motion. He begins the verse melody at varying pitch levels, depending on the emotional content of the text. Thus, in verses four and five (regarding the prison-like "cage" of the ship's hull and the terminal accident of Billy's father, respectively), the pitch level is higher and more intense.

The choruses, in typical Sting fashion, address the theme of escape. And, as expected, they use harmonic references to the relative major (F), a more hopeful key. The meter also "settles down" to a fairly straight-ahead 6/8, although Sting's melody still divides each measure into three. Billy's dream is that this ship would carry him and his father to the "Island of Souls." Sting mentions in an interview that this is a reference to the island of Lindisfarne (also known as "Holy Island"), which is just off the coast of Northumberland, north of Newcastle.[30] It is a tidal island, which at high tide becomes surrounded by the North Sea; but at low tide it is accessible by foot. At least in the context of this song (or in Sting's cosmology) it is also the legendary place where souls go when people die.

It is refreshing to hear the sarcastic, sneering Sting again. This is especially audible during verses four and five (as stated above), and has not been heard since "Synchronicity II." Over the course of the song, the rhythmic and background texture becomes more dense, and the "riveting" sounds of hammering steel and the like become more prominent. Along with Kirkland's ascending scales (first heard in the transition between the first chorus and verse four), this accumulation of sound gives the impression of a ship being built as the song progresses.

Another "accumulating" device that Sting builds into the song is the additive structure. The first verse is a typical quatrain (four-line stanza); the second is a quatrain with an extra line at the end and in a new key ("Billy would cry when he thought of the future"); the third verse has six lines, with the same chord progression for the fifth line as in the previous verse (cm-A♭), but then moving to B♭ for the sixth line. These last two lines might be thought of as the beginning of the chorus (since they are the same words and music both times they appear), but the extension of the initial fifth line and the overall smoothness between verse and chorus make it hard to draw a dividing line.

The two choruses also exhibit this additive quality. The first chorus is a typical quatrain again (although with a different rhyme scheme from the verse), but the second is extended by another rhyming couplet that delivers the title of the song as the last three words. The chart below summarizes the rhyme scheme of each verse and chorus and the number of lines:

Verse 1: abcb (4)
Verse 2: abcbc (5)
Verse 3: abcbdd (6)
Chorus 1: abcc (4)
Verse 4: abcbc (5)

Verse 5: abcbdd (6)
Chorus 2: abccdd (6)

A return of Tickell's small pipes (also present in the final chorus) leads us out of the song, amidst the cold north wind and a mysterious, mournful, watery groan. One of Sting's best songs is put to sea.

Then comes one of the greatest, most effective song transitions in Sting's catalogue: the exuberant, major key opening of "All This Time." This song, partially thanks to a cute video directed by Alex Proyas,[31] went to No. 5 on the Billboard charts. It is also one of the few solo Sting singles that use the sunnier major mode. This single really helped propel the album to No. 2, although it is not very representative of the album's general dark atmosphere.

What *is* representative are the lyrics. They tell of the death of another father; it is unclear whether the speaker is "Billy." It may not matter: What is relevant is that this father is dying by the sea, and rather than a formal church burial, the son wants to "bury the old man . . . at sea." This speaks to an anti-religious undercurrent on this album, which surfaces in several other songs. Other lines from this song address and critique religion as well, for example the father's directly sneering rejoinder to one of Jesus's Beatitudes (from Matthew 5) regarding inheriting the earth: "What good is a used-up world and how could it be worth having?" No wonder these priests are "fussing and flapping" nervously!

But through all of our human endeavors—and Sting includes religion in this category—the river flows eternally. It has been flowing since the time of the Romans, and it will flow hundreds of years from now. Sting uses the tried-and-true metaphor of the river transporting the dead to the afterlife (or, literally, the ocean) to allow the speaker (or "Billy") to grieve alone and not in a congregation (as in a burial service). This is further evidence of Jung's influence on Sting. Jung was not anti-religious, but he believed that the stories and archetypes that exist in the "collective unconscious" transcend religion and show us the interconnectedness of all people, no matter their religion. Basically, Sting is saying in "All This Time" that, for Billy (and for him), religion and empires are human constructions and will eventually fall away, but the eternal, primal fact of death will continue forever.

The way that the happy, sunny music interacts with and subverts the text is fascinating. The song follows a typical alternating verse-chorus pattern, with the chorus beginning on an e minor chord as opposed to the G major of the verse. It is a fairly standard harmonic pattern for the verses, dealing with the "earthly" matters of the fussing priests and the skeptical father. But then, when we get to verse four, the music modulates up a step (to A). The melody and vocal delivery are different enough from the previous verses that it initially sounds like a middle-eight section. But when the chorus comes back (also in A), we "rehear" the previous section as a fourth verse. This is another example of what I call a "hidden modulation" (cf. my discussion in chapter 3), and it is a transcendent moment.

For this verse is the crux of the song: It is at a higher level of reasoning and thus is at a higher pitch level. It is as if we have left the mundane world of last rites, priests, and human tradition (and G major) and have entered a higher level of consciousness and larger worldview (in A major). In this way it resembles an ideal music theater song: a song that effects and displays a transformation in the character or speaker, and over the course of the song the music is transformed as well.

"Mad about You" is based on an Old Testament story of King David, specifically the account of his infatuation with Bathsheba (2 Samuel 11). This story of obsessive love ends with David impregnating her, even though she is married to a soldier in his army. David has Uriah, the soldier, killed by sending him to the front line of the current war. What is most compelling about this tale is that it is not so much a story about adultery as it is about guilt. David deals with the consequences of his actions—indeed the angel Nathan encourages him to do so in order to remain a righteous man. As Sting writes in his introduction to the song in *Lyrics by Sting,* "punishment comes in Chapter 12";[32] the child conceived by Bathsheba falls ill and dies.

Whether Sting chose this topic for autobiographical reasons or simply that it follows his common theme of obsessive love is a matter of speculation. What is interesting is that Sting positions the song "in the moment"—that is to say, in the middle of David's decision making about whether or not to seduce Bathsheba. Given the way late twentieth-century rock stars are often seen by adoring fans, it might not be unthinkable to speculate that Sting might have occasionally found himself in a similar position. This speculation could be fueled by his admission that he was not entirely faithful to his first wife, Frances; moreover, this song dates from the period between his marriages. Is it possible that this song is both a song of mourning and of exorcising demons? Regardless, it is a "masculine" song about lust and thus fits well into this album's predominant focus on male experiences.

Sting was trying to suggest an ancient, Mediterranean sound in this song; he was only partially successful. The opening guitar pattern is passably Middle Eastern, but when the full band enters it feels like we're right back in a modern digital studio. If there is one song on this album that could be called "overproduced," this would be it. The texture is thick with synthesized flute, strings and piano, percussion, and bass and drums, along with Miller's guitar pattern. To me, the sonic landscape doesn't evoke a moonlit walk in ancient Judea, but rather a busy marketplace with many things going on simultaneously. Perhaps Sting was trying to emulate David's conflicted state of mind, but this is not apparent.

As a song about obsession, it is not as effective musically as "Every Breath You Take," where the repetitive nature of the chord and guitar pattern really captured the speaker's state of mind. "Mad about You" does not have as compelling a chord progression to make the repetitions work. On the other hand, the middle-eight section is a nice contrast to the minor-mode remainder of the song. This is the portion of the song that mentions love, so it is fitting that it is set apart.

After a repeat of verse one (implying that David's state of mind has not changed since the beginning of the song), there is a "summary" chorus, which combines one new line with two lines from the two previous choruses. The point is driven home three-fold (over three statements of the chord progression) that David would give up everything he has to be with Bathsheba. This type of summary chorus (or verse) at the end of a song is a technique also championed by, among others, Lucinda Williams.[33]

Another one of the few up-tempo songs on *The Soul Cages* is "Jeremiah Blues (Part I)." This song is a fun swing number that was mostly written during the recording sessions (in Paris and Migliarino, Italy).[34] It is a Jeremiah-like rant against the contemporary society of the early 1990s. Jeremiah was an Old Testament prophet who prophesied the destruction of Jerusalem and other calamities to befall the Israelites. But no one wanted to hear what he had to say. In being proved right, he then probably wrote the book of Lamentations to pour out his rage against God and his fellow Israelites.

Sting's lyrics are not so much warnings as sarcastic characterizations of the problems of the day. This song was written during the build-up to the Gulf ar (the United States began taking back Kuwait from Saddam Hussein on January 15, 1991, a week before this album was released). Margaret Thatcher, Ronald Reagan's conservative counterpart in the UK, was forced out of office in December of 1990.[35] There are many possible interpretations of some of the song's lines in the context of the early 1990s, but I think Sting deliberately stays general. Many of the problems and scandals mentioned could be taken out of today's newspapers as well.

A universal element that Sting uses is the idea of a scapegoat. The chorus mentions tying a "thief to a tree" and then follows with the enigmatic lines "sometimes I stare, sometimes it's me." Scapegoats, whether they be individuals or groups of people, have been used down through the ages to lay blame for society's ills. We humans have a simultaneous fascination with and revulsion for violence, and "sometimes it's me": any of us might persecute, or even become, the victim.

While this song is by no means a "blues," it does reference the rhythm-and-blues style, especially in Miller's screaming guitar. Structurally, it is essentially two verses with choruses in between. In the middle of the choruses (which begin in a very foreign key to the home key) there are a couple of strange, atonal interludes, the first by Kirkland, the second by Marsalis. These might represent the "something wicked this way comes" from Shakespeare's *Macbeth*. They remind me of a similar "bottom dropping out" effect of the breaks in "Synchronicity II."

The disappointing thing about this track is that Marsalis's playing seems to be an afterthought. He never gets a good lick in and seems to be overpowered by Miller's guitar work. In light of the fact that, after this track, Marsalis does not play much on *The Soul Cages,* and indeed has less and less of a presence on Sting's later albums,[36] "Jeremiah Blues" could be thought of as a "passing of the torch" of Sting's sidemen, from Marsalis to Miller.

Next comes another beautiful but sad Sting song, "Why Should I Cry for You?" This track draws its influence from fellow Englishman and successful solo artist Peter Gabriel. Gabriel's 1986 album *So* won multiple Grammys and proved that non-Western popular music (or "world music") was not only viable in the music industry but was becoming a major element in contemporary pop. "Why Should I Cry for You?" is not overtly world-music influenced, but it contains a mildly African flavor in its groove and percussion instruments.

Strip away the world-beat feel, however, and you get a beautiful, straightforward English folk-style song. In this song, it is difficult to distinguish between "verse" and a "chorus," which suggests a ballad-like strophic structure. A strophic song is one that usually lacks a chorus; in other words, the song is completely made up of verses that follow the same chord progression and generally the same melody. Often folk songs that use this form are "story songs," like "John Henry." "Why Should I Cry for You?" contains a refrain (also the title) that happens only twice: at the halfway point and towards the end, just before the coda.

There is not much variation in the harmonic progression ($A\flat$ $D\flat$/F $D\flat$, repeated three times, $A\flat$/C $D\flat$ $E\flat^{sus4}$ $E\flat$), except in verse five (beginning with "sometimes I see your face"). In verse four, right after the first refrain, Sting's vocal begins up an octave, and he changes the shape of the melody to a descending arc as opposed to an ascending one. This high $A\flat$ turns out to be the vocal high point of the song. We end this track with a pretty joyful vamp, based on the same music as the introduction but with a stronger organ presence by Kirkland. Sting plays a more animated bass lick, and one of the percussionists does a Brazilian-influenced vocalization.

All of this beautiful music making belies the text, however. In the grand concept of the album, this song fits in with the death of Billy's father. Billy is perhaps a sailor on a northern boat, "hauling on frozen ropes." The Faroe Islands, mentioned as the setting of the song, are in the extreme north of the North Sea and belong to Denmark, and the frozen north is used as a metaphor for Billy's icy state of mind. Almost all the verses contain rhetorical questions about truth, love, and death. Billy seems to be in the denial stage of grief, not wanting to answer any of the questions he asks himself. "Why Should I Cry for You?" is a rather defensive question. So either Billy did not love his father (unlikely) or he is in this denial place.

Another aspect that ties into the rest of the album is the atheistic (or perhaps agnostic) quality of the lyrics. In some ways the speaker is hopeless—adrift on a boat on the northern seas, lost because "the stars seem to lose their place." The dark angels that follow him are from the past; perhaps they represent guilt or leftover resentment. And the detail that they are flying over a "godless sea" implies that God is very far away from Billy at this point in the grieving. It is interesting to note that, over the course of the lyric, the question marks become increasingly prominent; so much so that the song ends with nine questions in a row. Many agnostics, as well as deeply spiritual people, have more questions than they do answers.

What makes this song problematic is that the music is calm, confident, gorgeous, and suggests a much happier theme. It is almost as if, in the joyous coda, Billy is happy that his father is dead. I doubt this is the effect Sting intended. Perhaps it is that he wanted the music of the coda to answer all the rhetorical questions; so the unspoken answer to the title question is "because I loved you." In this way, this song has a similar text/music conflict as "Every Breath You Take."

"Saint Agnes and the Burning Train" is a wonderful little instrumental that serves as a transition between the two halves of the album. This little waltz in e minor features Miller on the guitar melody and is refreshingly "clean" in its production: Only guitar, bass, and synthesizer are included. The song's structure follows a typical verse/chorus-middle pattern, with a short concluding coda. The end of the second "chorus" has the bass alternating B and C several times, which relates back to the opening phrase of the melody.

The track has a "continental" feel, and so it is somewhat surprising to learn that it is dedicated to his indefatigable paternal grandmother, Agnes Sumner. Sting tells the story[37] that she was traveling to one of his performances (which she did every chance she could), when the train she was on caught fire. This short song was written in honor of her indomitable spirit. What would, on another album, be considered a good candidate for a B-side works perfectly as an interlude and fits an album exploring Sting's heritage.

We seem to be immediately cast back into the sea with a recall of the concluding groan of "Island of Souls." The opening wash of sound of "The Wild Wild Sea" recalls mid-1970s progressive rock bands, such as Yes and Genesis, when they wanted an effect of subtly changing stasis. In many cases, this kind of gesture represented the ocean, as it does here.[38] Essentially two chords alternate over a static dissonant bass note. Katché plays cymbal rolls, commonly used to suggest foaming surf.

Of course, it is not simply the ocean that Sting is suggesting, but also the unconscious mind. Jung's "collective unconscious" is often represented in his writings as an ocean: deep, mysterious, unified, and representing our origins. Since Sting writes, in *Lyrics,* that this song was inspired by a dream,[39] it makes sense that we the listeners "enter into the song" through the collective unconscious of the ocean. The image also connects with the other sea-based songs on *The Soul Cages.*

"The Wild Wild Sea," like "Why Should I Cry for You?" is patterned after an English ballad, with no choruses. There are two main chord patterns that accompany each stanza, with slight variations in order to make transitions smooth. But what is more noticeable and relevant in a ballad-style song such as this is the variation in the vocal line. The vocal pattern generally follows the harmonic one; that is, the melody changes when the harmonic pattern changes. Sting's vocal register, naturally, follows the emotional content of the stanza. In true storyteller fashion, the lines describing the storm are at a higher, more exciting level.

This song has a gradual build (after the introduction) all the way to the final stanza, which nicely mirrors the increasingly close point of view of the speaker. At first he starts on the beach, and then he swims out, somehow gets aboard a ship, and sees his father steering the ship.

The fantastic imagery and strange events are explained by the speaker's dream. The dream itself does not start until stanza three, when he sleepwalks down to the beach. In dreamlike fashion, he swims with "the moon and her lover" and then suddenly and inexplicably finds himself aboard the ship that he thinks he saw in the first stanza. Another common occurrence in dreams is that of "waking up," which this speaker does in stanza six. But has he really woken up? He is still on the mysterious ship, and a storm is coming. Eventually he discovers that his father is trying to control the boat in the face of this mighty storm. A distant recall of Tickell's Northumbrian pipes, along with the watery groan, suggests that this is the same ship that was built and launched in "Island of Souls."

In Jungian analysis, as previously mentioned, the sea is a symbol of the unconscious mind. In this song/dream, the speaker finds himself aboard the vessel without knowing how he got there, and the ship is being guided by his father. This is possibly a symbol of being born and finding yourself in a family and, consequently, in a father-son relationship. The father as captain could be interpreted as the raising of the child, but at the mercy of the elements (in this case, the storm). The father does the best he can to weather the storm, which of course agitates the sea (the unconscious) and endangers the lives of both father and son.

In this light, in this song I believe Sting (or the speaker/Billy) is coming to terms with his relationship with his father. Ernie Sumner did the best he could, raising a family on a milkman's salary and sending his eldest son, Gordon, to grammar school (on a scholarship). Sting has also said that he felt extremely guilty for not attending either of his parents' funerals (which led to the writing of *Broken Music*).[40] He and Ernie had a contentious relationship, and they may not have patched things up completely before he died. "The Wild Wild Sea" may be Sting's way of acknowledging and honoring his father through the dream-state of songwriting and sailing on the seas of the collective unconscious.

The title track, which earned Sting the "Best Rock Song" Grammy in 1991 (his fifth), comes next. It's a pretty heavy rock sound for Sting, who hadn't done a song this rocking in a very long time (perhaps "Synchronicity II," but most "rocking" Police songs are much faster). This quality was probably influenced by Dominic Miller's guitar work, being an alum of the band World Party and having worked with several other rock bands through the 1980s. This song is also riff-based, which makes it stand out from other songs on the album.

The lyrics concern the well-known British legend of "Davy Jones's locker." This phrase is used as a euphemism for dying at sea. To be "put into" the locker or chest that lies at the bottom of the ocean is to die by drowning. According to the legend of Davy Jones, the keeper of the locker or "soul cages" is a kind of demon of the sea; in Sting's song he is personified as an old fisherman. If a sailor encounters him, in the song's version, he must challenge him to a drinking contest. If the sailor wins, the keeper sets the captive souls—or a single soul—free; if the sailor loses, he becomes a captive himself.

At the end of the song it appears that the "boy child" (Billy) wins the wager: "one less soul in the soul cages." What is unclear is if this soul is the soul of the father. That seems to be implied by the recall of the final stanza of "Island of Souls."[41]

As stated above, "The Soul Cages" is heavily riff-based. Miller's riff serves as the introduction and the chorus. Most of the musical material is based on this idea. The sections that are not are a brief "middle," serving as a transition to the first chorus without recurring in the song, and a short saxophone break that starts a step up, on A, serving as the first "hidden modulation" (similar to "All This Time," but far less effective). So, the first three verses use the riff in g minor, and then we have the middle, and then a chorus. After the sax break we have three more verses and a chorus in the new key of a minor. Then, for the crucial, previously mentioned (and confusing) verse seven, we once again have a verse in the same key of a minor, though combined with the chorus riff.

For the last part of this next chorus, Sting adds a descending bass line, which leads nicely into the recall of "Island of Souls." This recall is played a third higher than the original (in f♯ minor), giving Sting's voice more urgency here. After yet another reference to the soul cages chorus, the song fades. The resulting harmonic arc of this song is thus: g minor, a minor, f♯ minor, outlining a large-scale descent of a half-step.

For me, this song does not work as a unifier to close out (or almost close out) this concept album. Partly to blame is the lack of melodic interest in the voice part, but the guitar riff also gets old rather quickly and does not gain any new quality in the new keys that it is played in. The crucial verse seven is not highlighted musically (which adds to the confusion) and the song ends a half-step lower than it began, possibly leading to a "deflated" feeling in the listener. Moreover, stylistically it doesn't seem to fit: a bluesy rocker telling a story about Davy Jones's locker? Where's the connection?

Closing out this "somber collection of songs," as Sting describes them,[42] is "When the Angels Fall." This beautiful slow number shares a sound world with the mysterious "Tea in the Sahara" from *Synchronicity*. The subject matter, however, is far darker than that relatively slight lyric. The current of agnosticism or anti-religion on this album resurfaces here. Angels, crosses, churches, and even a pipe organ-like sound towards the end: All of these organized-religion referents are addressed in the coda's statement of "You can't control us anymore."

It is helpful to consider this song as a partner to "All This Time." In that song, Sting's ultimate point was to search for something beyond organized religion in dealing with his father's death. It was not religious, but it was spiritual. "When the Angels Fall" is similar in that the speaker wants to dismantle the idea of angels—those characteristically Christian images of perfection that do not represent actual people—watching over us. On the other hand, during the marvelously quiet coda to this song, Sting sings "Peace on Earth" and "Joy to all mankind," which is what the angels say to the shepherds in the Christmas story (Luke 2:14). So perhaps in Sting's view there is room for the messages that angels bring but not for the traditional, supernatural image of angels with wings and harps.

It is a rich text, as many of the songs on *The Soul Cages* are. It is perhaps the closest together Sting's two worlds of Christianity and Jungian philosophy have come in one song (another is "Dead Man's Rope" from *Sacred Love*). The cross that leaves a "shadow" on the wall (which can happen as the paint around an object fades) also calls to mind the Jungian concept of the shadow of the self: everything that person is or thinks he is not. One of the goals of self-realization for Jung is to acknowledge and be in touch with this shadow. Otherwise it can come out in dangerous ways. The cross on the wall, then, needs to be acknowledged and not suppressed, even though Sting is uncomfortable with the trappings of religion.

Similarly, the ruined churches (implying the German bombing of English churches and towns in WWII) are still visited by shuffling people, searching for something to hold onto. I believe Sting is saying that we all need some sort of spirituality and connectedness with a higher plane but that people also need freedom of thought and self-realization.

"When the Angels Fall" shares a key center of G with "All This Time," "The Wild Wild Sea," and the first part of "The Soul Cages." Similarly to "The Wild Wild Sea," it fluctuates between G major and g minor. Specifically, the first half of each of the two verses as well as the coda are centered in G major, and the second half of the verses and coda are in g minor.

What makes this a surprisingly hopeful song (despite the slow tempo) is the coda. Here we have moved out of the chorus (or introduction) from a c minor chord, as we did the first two times, into G major. But this time we *stay* in G major, a fact made plain and seemingly inevitable on the last syllable of "anymore." In classical music theory, this moment is termed a "confirmation" of a key—a point at which the piece of music seems to know that it's in this key, despite the fact that it may have touched that key earlier in more tentative ways. This is also an incredibly important moment in the key relationships of the album as a whole. It confirms "G" as the main tonal center of the album and offers hope for escape from the soul cages, suggesting that Sting has worked through his demons.

So Sting's most overt "concept album" can be seen as fulfilling personal and financial goals (it was yet another No. 1 album in the UK) but falls a bit short of his artistic capabilities. My feeling is that it could have been a truly great album, but there are a couple problem songs ("Mad about You," "Jeremiah Blues," and "The Soul Cages") that weigh the brilliant ones down. The major problem for me is that the title song fails to live up to its function as a unifying piece. It doesn't succeed lyrically or musically in the ways his best songs do.

A promotional shot from around 1980. From left: Andy Summers, Stewart Copeland, and Sting. Courtesy of Photofest.

Sting as the devilish Martin Taylor in *Brimstone & Treacle* (1982). Courtesy of Photofest.

Sting in 2001. Courtesy of Photofest.

The Police in full concert mode, circa 1981. Courtesy of Photofest.

The Police as superstars, circa 1984. Courtesy of Photofest.

On the set of David Lynch's epic science fiction film *Dune*, filmed in Mexico City. Once again, Sting played an evil character. The film's release in the summer of 1984 helped keep him in the public eye even after the *Synchronicity* tour ended. From left: Sting, Lynch, and Kyle MacLachlan. Courtesy of Photofest.

Sting onstage at the Théâtre Mogador in Michael Apted's film *Bring on the Night* (1985). From left: Darryl Jones, Sting, and Branford Marsalis. Courtesy of Photofest.

Sting performing a new version of "Roxanne" for the first time with The Police since 1986, at the 49th Annual Grammy Awards, February 2007, in Los Angeles. Courtesy of Photofest.

Return

After touring the world for most of 1991 and early 1992 (including a poignant return to his hometown of Wallsend), Sting moved his family from the house in Highgate to a giant manor house in Wiltshire (near Stonehenge) called Lake House. He says that the fresh air and country life really inspired him to write happier, more playful songs.[1] *Ten Summoner's Tales* was the result. Released in March of 1993, it reached No. 2 on the Billboard album chart, buoyed by a couple of top-40 singles ("If I Ever Lose My Faith in You" and "Fields of Gold").

The album title is a pun on Sting's last name, Sumner. A summoner was the holder of a medieval occupation that involved bringing people into court for trial or to be a witness. It is also what the name Sumner is derived from. In Geoffrey Chaucer's *The Canterbury Tales,* there is a "Summoner's Tale," which is a satirical and vulgar tale about a friar who visits a sick man and wants the man to feed him a grand meal. The offended sick man avenges himself by farting on the friar; it is essentially a childish payback for the previous tale, "Friar's Tale," which insulted the summoner.

This tale has nothing to do with Sting's album, except that it hints that this will be a fun collection of varying songs (much like Chaucer's book is a collection of varied stories). As Sting says, his primary goal was to entertain.[2] It is hard to imagine a larger change from the introspective concept album approach of *The Soul Cages.* Even the album art is more cheery, with several attractive shots of Sting taken at Old Wardour Castle in Wiltshire.[3]

Ten Summoner's Tales' core band consists of the musicians Sting worked with the most on the previous *Soul Cages* tour: In addition to Miller, he used drummer Vinnie Colaiuta and keyboardist David Sancious. The new band plays on all songs, with additional musicians brought in as needed. The band is in top form for the opening track, "If I Ever Lose My Faith in You," which reached No. 17 on the Billboard Hot-100 chart. The hip-hop-inspired groove laid down by Colaiuta seems to be deliberately "updating" Sting's sound, proving that he can remain relevant with a changing audience. In the early 1990s, grunge had taken over many AOR stations' playlists, but hip-hop was coming to the fore as a major style in the rest of the pop world. The hip-hop influence here is purely the swing rhythm, which Sting had not overtly used since "Shadows in the Rain" on *The Dream of the Blue Turtles.*

This song is one of Sting's "list" songs, where a central idea (usually the title) is given and the verses consist of examples of this idea. Another example of this type of lyric is "King of Pain." The words do not tell a story or change over the course of the song. Here, the verses are used to list the corollary of the chorus: what Sting *has* lost his faith in—science, religion, government, the military, even game-show hosts. But the chorus regulates this and implies that he will never lose his faith in the person he loves. It's a love song of disillusionment. This is the second time that he has referenced game-show hosts. The first time was in the liner notes to . . . *Nothing Like the Sun,* comparing them to televangelists. Here, he's mockingly comparing them with politicians (Bill Clinton, in the 1990s, did bear a striking resemblance to several game-show hosts!).

The music for "If I Ever Lose My Faith in You" was probably written on the guitar. There are many moments and chords that make more sense on a guitar than on a piano. For example, all of the chords of the chorus have Miller striking the top two strings (B and E), no matter if they are "part of the chord" or not. Also, several chords make use of the "suspension" harmony figure, which can best be heard in the verses at the beginning of each chord change. Both of these techniques create a mildly dissonant, beautifully rich texture underlying Sting's vocals.

This song is quite interesting harmonically. There seem to be two keys competing for dominance: A and E. The verses (as well as the short introduction) center on A, and the choruses, the list part of the middle, and coda all hover around E. The characteristic bass pattern of both the choruses and the second part of the middle is of ascending steps (somewhat foreshadowed by the rising internal line of Sancious's keyboard in the introduction). This ascending pattern normally happens on E in the choruses but also happens on f♯ (in the middle) and B (in the final extended chorus).

The rising pattern almost always consists of four chords; thus the bass moves up four notes from the starting pitch. In each appearance of the pattern, it is played twice. The lone exception to this is the middle, where the pattern starts on f♯. The second time through in this case, on the line "But every time I close my eyes, I see your face," the pattern only rises three chords and stays on A. This brief moment of stasis coincides with the speaker recalling his lover's face, in the midst of being lost in the lies of the outside world (and, metaphorically, "lost" in another key). It also triggers a new verse by simply restarting on the same chord of A.

The final choruses also use the chord pattern metaphorically. Here we get the title and its rhyming line with the chord pattern starting on B, and the vocal is sung down a fourth from the original. After two times in this foreign key (B, C♯, D, E), the pattern finds itself on E again, and we simply restart the chorus on that pitch. After a final suspension figure on the last chord in the pattern (A), we recall the e minor middle and fade. The last choruses thus seem to be finding their way back to the original key of the chorus (E) and finding their way back to faith. The e minor coda supplies the missing line of the chorus, because there is nothing left to do.

In this way, the key of the choruses (E) wins the battle, and faith overcomes the verses' non-faith, despite the competing and distracting other keys that the pattern appears in. This makes sense, since it is easier to lose faith in something (especially abstract impersonal things, like the government) than it is to keep faith. The verses are "easily" in A and never waver, while the choruses begin in two different keys before regaining the true one.

As if to let the listeners know right away that this is going to be an eclectic, carefree album, the second track, "Love Is Stronger than Justice (The Munificent Seven)" begins with Dominic Miller in "Classic Western Soundtrack" mode and leads into a complex 7/8 groove. This is already a musical joke, even before the silly lyrics begin. An Old West soundtrack in 7/8 played by Weather Report? Although this was an unlikely hybrid in 1993, it is now hard to remember just how surprising it was. This is also a song on which the new band certainly gets to display its chops, especially Colaiuta, who provides a wide array of fun and deliberately confusing snare hits throughout all four verses.

As Sting mentions in the introduction to this song in *Lyrics by Sting,* he was trying to graft together two stories that had the number seven in common: *The Magnificent Seven,* the 1960 classic Yul Brynner/Steve McQueen western, and *Seven Brides for Seven Brothers,* a 1954 Hollywood film musical starring Howard Keel.[4] Sting retains the gun-slinging hero story from the former but dispenses with the sugarcoated romance of the latter film. There is indeed one bride for the main character (as in the musical), but instead of finding brides for them all, he eliminates the brothers. The rhyming of "brothers" and "get rid of the others" is quickly and hilariously done, as the narrator easily dispatches them. Other rhymes in the song "Love is Stronger than Justice" make it clear that Sting is having fun with the lyrics: "Burritos" rhymed with "banditos," and "litres" with "señoritas."

The narrative grafting of these two stories (in essence creating a third) is echoed by the musical juxtaposition of the 7/8 choruses with the straight-ahead country chorus, complete with pedal steel guitar, played by Paul Frank-lin. The way these transitions happen is through a constant eighth note pulse. In the verses, the eighth notes are grouped into sevens, and in the chorus (when the meter shifts to 4/4), they are grouped into eights (or two groups of four).

The harmonic structure, perhaps because of the rhythmic complexity, is simple. The verses and introduction contain but one chord in a minor. The choruses, in a typical move, use the relative major and follow a deliberately "country" style three-chord progression. Another tongue-in-cheek musical joke happens during the second guitar break. The chord modulates up a step, as if Sting is doing one of his characteristic "hidden modulations." However, in a moment that seems to acknowledge that this is a playful song and not any deeper than that, the guitar melody brings the band back down to the original key of a minor for the final verse.

The sense of fun continues into the coda, with a great jam in 7/8 that I wish continued for longer. Sancious demonstrates his skill at keeping the band going while playing extremely spread-out chords and fusion-style licks. Unlike later songs in this country idiom, Sting's first foray into this style is humor-filled and satirical. My only criticism here is that, because it is a "story song" and he has a lot of information to impart, Sting must sing at a fast clip and some of the words get lost. In this way, it is similar to "Rock Steady" from . . . *Nothing Like the Sun*.

Next is the second top-40 hit from the album "Fields of Gold," which went to No. 16 on the Billboard chart. This beautiful, golden-colored song is many Sting fans' favorite of his solo career. It is essentially a newly com-posed folk song, with deliberately archaic turns of phrase, such as "among the fields of barley" and "for to gaze a while." "Fields of Gold" deftly combines sensuality with nostalgia and death, all in a very romantic (in every sense of the word) song.

The last two verses are situated in the "present" of the speaker's point of view. The song as a whole looks back to a time when the lovers gave them-selves to one another, and in the last verse it speculates about the speaker's own death. It is a beautiful meditation on life, love, the changing of the seasons, and death.

Since it is styled as a "folk song," Sting keeps things musically simple, with subtle variations in the harmonic pattern for the six verses. Kathryn Tickell adds an "English" flavor with her Northumbrian pipes at the ends of verses one and three. In verse three, Miller doubles Sting's voice with his acoustic guitar, and in verse four his arpeggios emulate the west wind. The middle section does not venture far off, but it's enough of a textual difference to provide a slight contrast to the purely strophic remainder of the songs. Here is a wisely constructed, simple but effective and mature love song.

"Heavy Cloud No Rain" seems to be another mature love song, specifi-cally from a man's perspective. Sting borrows a metaphoric technique from the blues tradition: weather patterns representing sexual urges, or the lack of them.[5] The songwriting gift that Sting has is evident in the way that, for most of the song, the subject is "innocently" weather and the need for rain. First, the speaker just wants it to rain; then we hear from the "royal astrologer" of Louis XVI (executed during the French Revolution), who hopes that rain would delay his guillotining, then a farmer, who needs rain for his crops and livelihood, and finally back to the speaker, who is told by his lover to wait for a "rainy day."

The groove and saxophone and organ-filled sound is reminiscent of "Rock Steady" as well of course of Stax-era soul. Sting himself may have been having flashbacks of *Ghost in the Machine,* with the use of multi-tracked saxophones in the background. Miller contributes a fabulous Stevie Ray Vaughn–inspired solo, which uses the same chords as the verse (am^7, Cm^{7+6}, D^7, am^7) and ends with the vocal refrain/title. This leads smoothly into the middle eight, which starts in the relative major chord of C. This middle section, instead of offering a sense of relief to the rest of the song, seems to imply a heightening of tension in the speaker. Sting does this by increasing the "harmonic rhythm" (the rate at which the chord changes happen), so that now there are eight chords in the space of 16 beats, whereas before there may have only been one or two. The final chord of this middle section is the only one of its kind in the whole song: It is the V^7 chord (E^7), the point of maximum polarity (or tension) to the tonic of a minor. This angst-filled moment occurs directly before the speaker propositions his lover. The final verse is shortened (or back to the original length of verse one), and only has one chord. The coda of alternating am^7 and cm^7 chords can be heard as a frustrated recall of the previous verses. This is a very sly and cleverly worked out song in which the meaning is underscored and amplified by the harmonic structure.

The fun continues in "She's Too Good for Me," another tongue-in-cheek song of frustration from a man's perspective. Most of this frantically paced song—at 2:30 it is the shortest song (excluding instrumentals) in Sting's solo catalogue—is in list form, which gives Sting plenty of room for playful rhymes. The verses use the colloquial working-class conjugation of "she don't," implying the class difference between the speaker and his love interest. Some of the couplets are wonderfully suggestive: "She won't let me go that far." This is a courtship song, which I believe is why the whole thing begins with a ticking clock. Beneath the "frantic" surface, however, there is a fairly normal song structure: three verse-chorus pairs with a (very) contrasting middle section before the final verse-chorus pair. In the middle section, the diction changes to a more refined syntax, but it quickly makes the speaker feel like he is not being true to himself. Apparently the couple stays together because of the "games" that they play. There is a possible implication that he means sexual games, but it could also mean the psychological and courtship games that can happen in the early part of a relationship.

The verses are essentially one chord (c minor), with the dissonant poly-rhythmic guitar figure from the introduction continuing throughout most of the song. The chorus uses a descending bass line to get down to G (on "play") and then return to C. Each chorus ends with a sudden stop (the final one marking the end of the song).

The middle section warrants a closer look. Extreme contrast is the point of this middle. Here we have a different key, a string quartet, a different verbal idiom, and a slower tempo. Moreover, the string quartet is arranged in the manner of a Beethoven slow movement; that is to say, in four-part counter-point. This section consists of four musical phrases, each pair of which gener-ally descends down to the V chord and then returns to tonic.[6] The middle section is what is known in the classical world as "tonally closed," meaning that, as a section, it begins and ends on the same chord (b♭m). It does not "travel" anywhere harmonically or take us to another key. In this way, Sting sets it apart as something separate from the rest of the song and thus separate from the true nature of the speaker himself.

Another playful courtship song follows, and it is one of my favorites. "Seven Days" has been compared by Christopher Sandford to an early Joe Jack-son aesthetic of a self-deprecating narrative voice who is vying for the affec-tions of a woman.[7] Sandford may have been thinking of Jackson's hit "Is She Really Going Out with Him?" which does share some qualities with "Seven Days." The most obvious similarity is the love triangle: a meek, perhaps nerdy speaker and a big, muscular dunderhead, both after the same woman. What is different is that, here, the woman has given the speaker (and, possibly, the Neanderthal) seven days to win her hand. She is forcing the issue to make this hesitant suitor commit to her. The song's 5/8 time signature keeps things awkwardly bouncy, and Colaiuta does some wonderful things with the groove. A fairly standard chord progression (although not without chromatic interest) makes up the verses. The chorus features another one of Sting's chromatically ascending bass lines, which significantly avoids the home chord of C major—perhaps this illustrates the speaker's indecision and hesitancy.

The most revealing portion of the song is when the narrative voice goes deeper inside during the middle eight. Here, the narrator admits that he truly loves the woman and cannot run away. We feel that this is true because of the smoother, more introspective mood of these bars. Also, the harmony seems as if it is on another plane somehow. This passage, I believe, reveals the true feelings of the speaker, and since the coda uses the same C-B♭ alteration, a happy outcome is suggested. This coda contains yet another quotation of "Every Little Thing She Does Is Magic," which we have also heard in "O My God." The hesitancy and self-doubting feeling of courtship as illustrated in that first song fit perfectly in "Seven Days." But this guy will win. It's in the music.

Another love triangle is set forth in "Saint Augustine in Hell." This time, however, the other man is not the speaker's enemy, but his best friend. The main subject of this song is lust, not the love that we saw in "Seven Days." Lust is, of course, one of the traditional seven deadly sins. However, an even greater sin according to Dante in his *Inferno* is betrayal. The speaker here seems more than willing to betray his friend for a sexual liaison with this irresistible woman.

This would seem to be a song involving the traditional view of hell, with fire and devils with tridents. The middle interlude with David Foxxe's narration would seem to indicate that imagery. But, by placing the narrative of the song in contemporary society, and thereby making the narrator "alive,"[8] Sting is making a larger point. Many people that are still alive today are in their own hell, brought upon themselves by various "sins." They seem trapped in endless cycles, which is why Dante's hell is made up of concentric circles that the sinners are doomed to travel.

Sting depicts this circular nature of hell musically. Each verse outlines a progression that always returns to the home chord (am, F, E, F, am), and at the end of each chorus, we seem to slide back down into the muck. The asymmetrical meter of 7/8 also has a circular feel, especially with Sting's repetitive bass pattern and Colaiuta's cymbal work.

The music for the narrated middle section, which is adapted from Sting's B-side instrumental song "I Miss You Kate," is naturally contrasting with the frenzied rest of the song. It is in 3/4 and works perfectly as a kind of "lounge in hell" music, for the speaker's "break." Sting has the actor Foxxe get in some digs at his nemeses in real life: lawyers, critics, and accountants.[9] Next, a fiery organ solo by Sancious takes the place of a third verse, which may represent the two men fighting over the woman or even the death of the narrator. A final chorus and recall of the introduction closes out the song with an "eternal" fade.

The next song, "It's Probably Me," is the one disappointment on *Ten Summoner's Tales*. As Sting explains, he wrote the words to the pre-existing instrumental by film composer Michael Kamen and Eric Clapton for the movie *Lethal Weapon 3*.[10] He was asked to write a "buddy song" to fit with the film. It fits the bill, I guess, but the relationship between the two figures in the song (ostensibly the roles played by Danny Glover and Mel Gibson) feels quite thin, and this makes for an unconvincing song. The title itself implies a song about guilt. But Sting chooses (or was told) not to address this more interesting topic and instead to concentrate on the loyalty angle. I believe that if Sting had been given free rein on this commission he would have come up with something more believable and insightful.

Kamen and Clapton's music for the song is rather drab and monochromatic, with not enough contrast to keep things interesting. The muted trumpet that plays throughout is supposed to sound "cool," but it ends up getting old quickly and feeling hokey. This unknown player is not given a real solo, either; he's too low in the mix. Moreover, the middle section, which in a good Sting composition provides a welcome sense of contrast, does not differ enough from the chorus to be effective. It also does not have a contrasting mood in the text. If anything, "It's Probably Me," by its plain mediocrity, highlights Sting's talents as a songwriter on the rest of this album and in just about his entire solo catalogue.

The original soundtrack version of this song appears on the greatest hits collection *Fields of Gold*. It actually does a better job of providing contrast and interest. Eric Clapton and David Sanborn (alto sax) both have solos right before the third verse, and the recording also includes Kamen's string arrangement. Sting says that he wanted to record the song for *Ten Summoner's Tales* to give the album a more "nocturnal" feel.[11] That may have worked, but the above-mentioned elements were sacrificed because of it.

"Shape of My Heart" is a collaboration between Sting and Miller. Sting explains that it was Miller who came up with "a beautiful guitar riff,"[12] and then Sting added words to the music. In this way it was created through a process similar to the previous song, but with far better results. Perhaps it was the close proximity of the two songwriters that made a better product, but they also did not have any outside forces telling them what to do.

The origins of our standard deck of playing cards are closely related to the art of divination. The first card decks were what we now think of as Tarot decks, whose first mention dates to 1367.[13] The four Tarot suits of wands, swords, pentacles, and cups correspond to the modern-day clubs, spades, diamonds, and hearts. Ralph Metzner notes that they also are each connected to the four elements of fire, air, earth, and water.[14] These decks, with their rich history of symbolism, were used for both gaming and for divination. Jung himself was very attracted to the archetypal images associated with many of the cards.

As most unbiased contemporary Tarot readers believe, the act of "fortune telling" is much more about meditation and stillness—listening to what you didn't know you already knew—than it is about psychic or parapsychological power. The person for whom the cards are being read makes associations with the imagery and history of each card (often with the help of a guidebook to the symbolic history) that are relevant to that person's history and present emotional state. The various patterns and methods of laying down the cards use the element of chance to allow people to see their lives from different angles and to encourage them to find solutions to their questions and problems. A modern-day card reader is more of a psychotherapist than a mystical fortuneteller.

Sting takes this angle and creates a brief sketch of a man who is perhaps a card dealer or gambler as an occupation, or perhaps just a casual player. We can assume that he is a somewhat mournful soul who keeps to himself and secretly uses the cards to figure his life out. He is also apparently, as we learn in verse four, in love with someone.

Sting uses the metaphor of gambling and gaming to make larger points about life. Many successful people have taken risks that in some ways could be seen as gambles. People go to school and specialize in a field without know-ing for certain whether or not there will be a job for them in their field. Sting himself made the risky move to London, leaving behind family, friends, his band, and his teaching job to "make it" as a musician. He is quick to admit, as most successful stars are, that luck had much to do with his success.[15]

The last verse especially makes clear this connection between life, luck, and gambling. In the speaker's mind, people who talk while playing cards "know nothing," and "those who curse their luck in too many places" are perhaps putting too much weight on the game instead of on their own life choices. Yes, sometimes one is the victim of bad luck. But sometimes one creates problems for one's self that could have been predicted and avoided.

In "Shape of My Heart," Sting jumps between a third-person and a first-person perspective. The first three verses are third person, while the choruses and the last two verses are first person. This has the effect of going deeper inside the speaker's head as the song progresses. It also implies the "self-other" state of card playing. You know what is in your hand, but you can't (at first) know what is in the other players' hands.

This is a song that uses the same chord pattern for the verses and chorus. This type of song form is sometimes called "AAA" form.[16] In other words, the chorus is still a chorus in the traditional sense of using the same text and melody each time it returns, but the underlying chord progression is identi-cal to the verse. In this type of song, the chorus typically has a contrasting melody to the verse, as it does here.

Other ways that the chorus is differentiated are achieved through instru-mentation: double-tracked harmony vocals by Sting, a solo cello, and light keyboard sounds by Sancious. Larry Adler, in 1993 a septuagenarian veteran of the British jazz scene, contributes a haunting harmonica solo in place of verse four.[17] This iteration of the chord progression happens in a contrasting key (c♯ minor), which serves to break up the repetitive nature of the song. In fact, the constant repetition of the same 14-chord pattern calls to mind the repetitiveness of a card game with several hands.

"Something the Boy Said" fits into a long line of moody, enigmatic Sting songs. Its mysterious narrative is timeless and could be set in any century where there are armies and war. The speaker is a rank-and-file soldier who has a typical, but useful, fearless attitude towards the unknown. He feels safety in numbers and no fear for whatever the company is looking for (it is never named). The captain's son makes a dire prophecy that sticks with them every-where they go. The boy predicts that they will all die and be feasted upon by crows. And sure enough, it happens (somehow), and the speaker survives to tell the tale.

This very dark song has no clear metaphorical meaning, although its gen-eral themes are prophecy from an unexpected source (as it often is in classical tragedies), fear of the unknown, and mistrust of authority. We are not even sure what happened: The speaker at this point is more concerned with trying to make sense of the boy's prophecy. Or did he know something that the soldiers did not?

This song again showcases Adler on harmonica, adding to the lonely, desolate scene. It follows a standard structure of alternating verse-chorus with a short break for doubled harmonica and bass. The chorus (beginning with "every step we took today") begins on the relative major chord ($B\flat$)—implying an attempt to escape, as in past songs. But each time, the progression seems to gravitate back to g minor, back to the prophecy of doom that the boy spoke.

On this recording, Sting uses a five-string bass. This instrument has a string below the typical low E, and it is often tuned to B or C below that E. My suspicion is that for this song he tuned it to $B\flat$, which is the lowest note that he plays and can be best heard at the beginning of the first chorus.

It is only fitting that Sting closes out *Ten Summoner's Tales* with an eleventh track, the "Epilogue (Nothing 'Bout Me)."[18] It is fittingly upbeat, sunny, and tongue-in-cheek and is not without interest. Sting is often coy about how much his songs have to do with his personal life. In one sentence he might say that many people try to overanalyze him through his songs, but then in the next sentence he will say that maybe his songs do reflect his personality in some way. His playful side definitely comes out on this album, and "Nothing 'Bout Me" is but one more example of that. It is a response to his critics and his fans who try to get inside his head and "know" what he is thinking.

At the same time, it works as a song for all artists. It is tempting for us, the audience, to read too much into works of art, unless they are of the confessional variety. A good artist does not necessarily always feel that their voice or viewpoint is the only one worth hearing. Rather, the true artist must have a natural gift of empathy and be able to inhabit other viewpoints convincingly. One might argue that the present study itself reads too much into Sting's songs, but I have tried to keep my analyses focused on how the music expresses the text and consider each song on its own terms.

The same playful writer that is evident on songs like "She's Too Good for Me" shows up in rhymes like "pockets/sockets" and "computer/college tutor." The wonderful thing about this song is that one gets the sense that Sting is getting used to and becoming comfortable with fame. He knows that, figuratively at least, fans and the media all want to get a piece of him and rummage through his various houses. But even if they do, they cannot get at his core self. It is a song about privacy and the struggle to maintain it while staying true to oneself.

This song has the same tempo and groove (though not the same key) as the opening track. In that way, it bookends the album (literally, on the British version). It has a charming bass riff that easily supports the chord changes. The first refrain offers a hint of what is to come in the coda: a four-note bass pattern that is played twice. On the second refrain we hear this pattern three times. After a contrasting middle section featuring brass, Sancious's keyboard solo, and the final verse, we hear the refrain again, with the same four-note pattern. But after a repetition of the title phrase and the bass pattern repeated eight times, the song seems to begin taking off into the stratosphere. With a constant tonic note, the band rises and rises, seemingly forever, as the song and album fade away.

This type of ending is reminiscent of The Beatles' "I Am the Walrus" and, to a lesser degree, "A Day in the Life."[19] It exemplifies a mathematically related concept called a Shepard scale, in which the aural illusion of an infinitely ascending "ladder" of music is created. Basically, each voice in the structure always ascends, but they enter and exit unnoticeably. In Sting's song, after he plays the four-note pattern eight times, he ascends stepwise to an octave above the original pitch level. Meanwhile, the strings and keyboard keep playing ascending lines, and the brass section continues vamping on its earlier material.

This magical ending to the song implies, depending on the point of view, either that Sting is "ascending" away from us, the listeners, and is never quite graspable, or that the critics and investigators' attempts to pin him down and define him are evaporating into thin air. Either way, it is a positively buoyant ending and succeeds in Sting's stated goal of leaving us with smiles on our faces.[20]

FIELDS OF GOLD AND DEMOLITION MAN

Ten Summoner's Tales was enormously successful and helped put Sting back on the map and in the public eye. After the misunderstood doldrums of *The Soul Cages,* fans appreciated this new, reinvigorated Sting. The supporting tour, which took him from Europe to Singapore, lasted well into 1994. It seemed only natural to ride this wave of success with a greatest hits album. *Fields of Gold: The Best of Sting, 1984–1994* includes two new songs and alternate versions of older songs. The international version also included "Fragilidad" ("Fragile" in Portuguese) from the primarily Spanish-language EP . . . *Nada Como el Sol.*

"When We Dance" was the lead single from this collection, and it reached a peak Billboard position of No. 38. It is another love-triangle song, but a unique one in Sting's repertoire, and I would argue in the popular song repertoire at large. It is a love song to a married woman, whom the speaker believes is in an unhealthy relationship. He is willing to do almost anything (except violence, which is not mentioned) to win her hand. He obviously knows her as a "friend" and can only be close to her when they dance. This text is most likely all occurring within the speaker's head. This is similar to an opera aria, where time seems to be suspended in order for the character to express his or her feelings.

As in many of Sting's songs, there are several literary and biblical references. The first two verses liken the woman's marriage to a bargain with the devil.

This reference, possibly to the *Faust* story, was also seen in "Wrapped around Your Finger." Verse three (beginning with "The priest has said my soul's salvation") addresses the traditional Christian notions of sin and salvation based on the morals of the day. The implication is that the speaker would commit a sin and risk going to hell for this woman. The middle section seems to advocate a "post-religion" world, where the institution of marriage would be dismantled and heaven is right here on Earth (because the two would be together). So for this speaker, religion and marriage are inextricably linked. These ideas point forward to similar concerns that are dealt with on 2003's *Sacred Love*.

"When We Dance" has an interesting "bi-level" melodic organization. The hauntingly beautiful initial melody of the first two verses is echoed by the piano in verse three. Simultaneously, Sting sings a vocal countermelody in a faster rhythm. These two melodies can be heard side-by-side, played by the piano and organ, during a break after the second chorus. Next, Sting structures the remaining two choruses in a similar manner. After establishing the relatively slow chorus melody, another faster countermelody appears, almost like a mantra, with the lines "I'm gonna find a place to live." It is this mantra that returns to lead us into the final choruses (repeated three times) and also continues during the coda.

So these two levels of rhythm and melody represent the internal/external voicings of the speaker; the spoken and unspoken thoughts of this conflicted but hopeful man. Although both levels are addressing the married woman, the slow melodies of verses one and two and the chorus are things that could be said aloud, and the faster material connotes internalized thoughts that he doesn't feel he can verbalize (according to his moral code).

The middle section once again features a "hidden modulation," up a step, but here the new key does not get firmly established until the fourth verse starts. In other words, the middle does modulate up, but at the end of the section it moves back down to the original pitch level (of E). Once verse four begins, it moves back up (to F♯). In a typically expressive move, this middle, with its dream of dismantling cathedrals and the division between earth and heaven, uses an elevated key and provides contrast to the rest of the song. In this case, since most of "When We Dance" is a "soft" song, the contrasting part is loud. This makes sense, as the speaker is trying to break out of this situation that he feels trapped in.

Even though this is a song about being "stuck," because of the harmonic plan I feel that the final message is one of hope. After moving up a step for the last time in verse four, the new key "sticks," and the ensuing choruses are also at an elevated level. The last note of the chorus (on the word "dance") is at an even higher pitch than normal, accentuating the ascent of the speaker's hopes. Moreover, the "positive affirmation" mantra/countermelody continues underneath. The descending thirds in the bass line that first show up at the end of the second chorus now serve as the coda, which to me express pure joy and contentment.

Then, in a strange foreshadowing of a future song, Sting breaks into a new bass line, identical to that of "All Four Seasons" from his next album, *Mercury Falling*. This happens under the last four lines of the vocal part, which are practically whispered. Whether this is a deliberate foreshadowing or just coincidence is unclear. It is also possible that it is a musical quotation from an older song.

Another curious release from this period (1993) is the "mini-album" *Demolition Man*. It features a new arrangement of the 1981 Police track, from the movie of the same name starring Sylvester Stallone and Wesley Snipes and directed by Marco Brambilla. The disc also includes five live tracks recorded in Italy from the "Summoner's Travels" tour. The title track is a rather unsuccessful attempt to update the earlier song with backing vocals, samples, and an "industrial" sound. Nevertheless, this inclusion on a soundtrack pointed the way to several future film music projects that occupied Sting for the next 10 years. "All For Love," a 1993 collaboration with Rod Stewart and Bryan Adams, was written for the Disney production *The Three Musketeers,* starring Charlie Sheen and Kiefer Sutherland. The song, despite its schlocky, "power ballad" style, earned Sting his second No. 1 single.

A highlight of the live tracks from *Demolition Man* is a wonderfully playful version of "Love Is Stronger Than Justice." The band is the core quartet of *Ten Summoner's Tales:* Sting, Miller, Sancious, and Colaiuta. They seem to really click live, and each member has their moment to shine. This song is expanded to allow room for solos by Sancious and Miller. Sting's skill as a musician is easy to hear in his simultaneous singing and bass playing. The other live tracks are well done, and "It's Probably Me" is a combination of the original version with the album version, with an interpolation of "Sister Moon" tagged at the end.

MERCURY FALLING

Recorded during the summer and fall of 1995[21] and released in March 1996, *Mercury Falling* was the second major project that Sting recorded at Lake House, his Wiltshire home. While not as sunny or as successful as *Ten Summoner's Tales,* it contains some gems and further exploration of songwriting technique. Kenny Kirkland rejoined the band for this album, replacing Sancious. *Mercury Falling* reached No. 5 on the Billboard charts and No. 4 in the UK.

A major reason why this album did not fare as well as previous releases is that it did not have a "break-out" single, as every previous solo album of Sting's did. The highest position that any of the singles in the United States reached was No. 60 ("You Still Touch Me"). Despite this, two of the songs on the album were later recorded by country singers and fared quite well on the country charts. Moreover, with this album, Sting fulfilled a lifelong dream to record with real-life musicians associated with the Stax record label in Memphis, Tennessee. He hired the Memphis Horns (Andrew Love and Wayne Jackson) to play on four tracks. The Stax label was one of the most successful independent houses in history and virtually defined the soul sound of the 1960s and 70s. This music is also a lot of what Sting listened to as a grammar schooler: "If I look back to a golden age in my musical life, it probably coincides with the boom in soul music . . . that music means a great deal for me."[22]

A recurrent theme of *Mercury Falling* is that of aging, often represented by falling temperatures during the change of season (implied by the title). These two words open and close the album as a whole, appearing as they do at the beginning of the first track and at the end of the last track. Sting has said that the phrase for him is full of multiple meanings, including the previously mentioned falling thermometer reading, the planet moving through an astrological star chart, the planet itself setting in the sky, the winged messenger god finally slowing down, and Sting's own mercurial nature settling down.[23]

"The Hounds of Winter" opens the album on a somber note. The speaker, as we eventually learn, is a widower who is in mourning. He is trying to continue on with his life, and Sting includes some wonderful details to establish the mood, but he keeps hearing these mythical "hounds." What he is most likely hearing is the cold wind. But as many people (writers especially) have done for centuries, he ascribes an emotional state to the weather around him. We humans are metaphor-seeking creatures, giving meaning to natural phenomena or giving personalities to animals and the like.

The music for this song is built of four-chord phrases, pieced together in various configurations. Almost all of them contain a stepwise descending bassline, representing the "falling" of the speaker. The generally full-sounding opening (and similar ensuing sections) might represent the wind outside, and as soon as we enter the verse, we are "inside." By using the same chord progression, but simply at a softer volume and sparer instrumentation, Sting can really go into the thoughts of the speaker.

The chorus, even though its subject is his lost love, does not brighten the mood any. It remains staunchly in the home key of f# minor. The middle section (textless) provides contrast by starting on a different chord, but it also winds back to the home key by using the same last four chords of the chorus. This middle is then used after the last chorus as the underpinning of a Dominic Miller guitar solo. The song ends as bleakly as it began, with a snare drum roll fading away into the wind.

"I Hung My Head" occupies a similar place in Sting's work as "Love Is Stronger Than Justice," and it has the same track two slot of this album. They are both country songs put through the Sting filter of odd time signature and macabre humor. "I Hung My Head" is a shade darker than its companion piece, but it still has a quiet wit about it and is full of wordplay and irony.[24] Another "ballad"-type lyric, the refrain here is the title. It tells the story of a man who accidentally shoots and kills another man from a great distance, the guilt that he feels, and his subsequent hanging. The speaker in this song is the man who was executed. Sting states that the song grew out of the title;[25] probably from the pun of "hanging" one's head in shame, and of being hung by the neck. Another punning line is the first one: "Early one morning, with time to kill." In this first stanza the phrase means "time to waste." When this line is repeated as the first line of the last verse, however, it is literally "time to kill" the narrator.

The most interesting musical feature of this song is its asymmetrical meter. It is in 9/8, but it sounds sort of like a limping 4/4. The best way to understand it as you are listening is to count eighth notes out loud: "1–2, 1–2–3, 1–2, 1–2" (adding up to nine). Sting came up with the guitar pattern first,[26] and so this rhythm was most likely directly determined by this guitar riff.

Melodically and harmonically the song is straightforward. There is a varying third phrase of each verse, which largely is there to set up the last phrase to end on the tonic A. A ballad song like this needs breaks in the vocal line for variety and for the audience to let the words sink in. After verse two we get a break with the Memphis Horns and Hammond organ, and between verses three and four Kirkland takes an organ solo. The coda simply alternates the opening two chords of the riff, while Sting repeats the refrain several times.

One production detail that subtly illustrates the scene happens in verse four. During the previous verse and organ solo, Colaiuta plays full out and adds hits in a variety of places in the measure. This is after the first part of the song, in which he was rather reserved. During verse four, however, the drum volume gradually recedes and then comes roaring back towards the final refrain. This effect was probably created at the mixing board after the drum track was recorded. But in any event it has the wonderful effect of "zeroing in" on the rider in the distance that the narrator sees while on the gallows. It also recalls the sound of the similar spot in verse one.

One final comment: Because this song involved both a prominent guitar riff and the brass players, it was "tuned up" from A major to B♭ major. Miller's guitar (and possibly Sting's bass) was simply raised up a half-step so that his riff would be easy to play, and also so that the horns would play in the comfortable (for them) key of B♭. Retuning like this can also easily be done on a guitar using a capo—a moveable bar that can be attached to the fretboard to uniformly raise the pitch of all the strings. This was also likely the case for the next song, "Let Your Soul Be Your Pilot."

This song owes a heavy debt to Stax and Motown-era rhythm and blues. The participation of the East London Gospel Choir lends a distinctly soulful feel. Gerry Richardson, Sting's partner from his Last Exit days in Newcastle, also plays organ on this song. "Let Your Soul Be Your Pilot" was the first single from the album and was far more successful in the UK (No. 15) than in the United States (No. 86). The large-scale picture is fairly standard for a Sting song: verse-chorus alternation, with a middle section before the final verse. The last chorus is somewhat extended, with a brief "borrowing" of chords from the introduction. What makes this song a bit unique is the coda, which ends the song in the minor mode, not major like we started in. I think that this ending represents the difficulty of life's journey: It is not always going to be as easy as the first part of the song would have us believe. In this respect, it shares the sentiment of Peter Gabriel's "Don't Give Up," which ends with a minor key coda, as if exhorting the listener to "get to work." Sting relates that "Let Your Soul Be Your Pilot" was inspired by a friend of his who has AIDS but was facing the disease with courage and bravery: "It's a song about death, or dealing with death in a way that offers some sort of hope."[27]

Some critics have leveled charges of "pop psychology" and "hollow plati-tudes" at Sting for this song,[28] but it falls in line with his belief in the Jungian idea of individuation. "Let Your Soul Be Your Pilot" is a more mature, wiser response to "The Wild Wild Sea" or some of the earlier navigation-themed songs in Sting's output. It is about finding one's true nature without rely-ing on the baggage of contemporary mores or the distraction of external circumstances. So it is a welcome song of reassurance after the first two dark vignettes.

Next comes a track that is unique to Sting's catalog: "I Was Brought to My Senses" is really two songs fused into one. The two sections are quite differ-ent from one another, in key and time signature, style, and mood. This fits the text, because it mirrors the difference between evening and the following morning, describing an awakening in the speaker. The first stanza has the first mention of the Newcastle area ("the banks of Tyne") in his songs since *The Soul Cages.*[29]

"I Was Brought to My Senses" is a love song in the tradition of the Roman-tic poets, who often sought inspiration from nature and found symbols of their love in the natural world, not to mention the therapeutic benefits. Per-haps this is why Sting thought of quoting Tennyson: "If nature's red in tooth and claw" (from *In Memoriam*). The blood that is inherent in this line is likely connected to the "wounds" in the next few lines. The assumption is that nature is the "she" who wounded him, our speaker. And the wounds will also heal him (from some other affliction of the spirit). This is reminiscent of the imagery in "The Lazarus Heart." Nature is often gendered as female, as in "Mother Nature." It is fitting, then, that Sting makes this relationship between these two songs.

As mentioned above, this song radically changes after the initial "English folk ballad." After three verses of a relatively simple melody in D mixolydian mode (that are doubled by guitar and Tickell's fiddle), we suddenly shift into 7/8 and a Brazilian-inspired feel. This groove serves as a transition to the new key of G major and introduces the upcoming verse's chord progression. The chorus begins on the relative minor chord and uses elision to go back to the verse progression. Elision is a musical and poetic term that denotes a phrase that ends at the exact moment that a new one begins (usually with a chord or a word). Sting also uses this technique on the repetition of the chorus at the end of this song. The end of one chorus becomes the beginning of the next. The coda and fade-out features a welcome solo by Branford Marsalis, another old friend.

Next comes a somewhat disappointing song about loneliness and lost love, "You Still Touch Me." It is supposed to be soulful, opening with a guitar quote from "Soul Man" by Isaac Hayes and with the Memphis Horns, but they are not given much to do. However, there is definitely a Stax/Otis Redding feel to it. There is no real chorus, just a refrain of the title words. There is a contrasting middle section, but Sting's vocal rhythm is exactly the same as in the verses. The total effect of these seemingly small musical details is that the song seems to drag on, not developing or sustaining the listeners' interest. The most interesting chord pattern does not happen until the coda, when the speaker's continued loneliness seems to drag him down, in both pitch level and tempo. Frankly, it speaks to this album's overall lower quality that this was the most successful American single.

Since Sting has often spoken of his desire to break down the divisions between musical genres, it should not be surprising to learn that the music industry sometimes does not know where to place him. Rock? Pop? Adult contemporary? Jazz? Country? Dance? Any of these categories could work for particular songs. The next song on *Mercury Falling*, "I'm So Happy I Can't Stop Crying" in a later version with Toby Keith reached No. 2 on the Billboard country chart. Sting was still marketable, perhaps just not through the usual channels. (Sting's original version barely cracked the top 100 at No. 94.)

This song is a true Sting gem. Upon first listening, one might notice the change of key in the middle and how the last verse and chorus sound a bit brighter somehow, but beyond that it seems on the surface to be a "simple" country song. I will argue that nothing could be further from the truth. At a fundamental level, it has three verses and refrains, a middle eight, and then a final verse and refrain pair in the new key. But the musical and textual interconnections are quite complex, and I believe Sting has invented his own song form. Please refer to figure 5.1 below for the following discussion.

After a brief introduction, the vocal part begins with what we think is the first verse. We have no reason to think otherwise at this point. It doesn't *sound* like a chorus or refrain. The problem from an analytical perspective is that these first four lines use the same harmony and melody as the refrain/title. Thus I have called this first section an "expository refrain." It is expository because it and another later refrain share a similar function. In just a few lines, Sting delineates the situation: The speaker's wife has left him for another man and has custody of the children. It is a fairly recent separation, and the man is still trying to make sense of his life. Here Sting follows his own advice: "Sometimes you have to tell a huge amount of information in one line."[30]

Figure 5.1
Structural Diagram of "I'm So Happy I Can't Stop Crying"

Intro

                            Expository Refrain (R)

       Verse 1

                            R

       Verse 2   F♯ major

                            R

       Verse 3

                            R'

                            Middle

       Middle verse

· ·

                            Expository Refrain 2   G major
                            (R2)

       Verse 4

                            R'

Sting offers a quite good discussion of "I'm So Happy" in the *Lyrics* book.[31] To amplify what he has already said there, each of the verses has a different focus of people that radiate out from the central character. In order, they are his wife, his friend, and his lawyer, and in the middle section he is alone. In the last verse he finds communion with other "Sunday fathers" and also meets the friend again. This is why each of the expository refrains is related in my analysis: They both use four lines to set up the situation; that of the whole song and that of the narrator's newfound acceptance.

As Sting mentions, the key change is used to illustrate this man's change of heart. It is noteworthy that Sting says that the last verse and chorus:

> . . . if not exactly joyful, [are] meant to evoke possibility, a glimmer of hope for the future. He has lost his cynicism, and this change of heart is illuminated by the key change—half a step—and the world keeps on turning.[32]

Many of Sting's previous modulations (key changes) are of a whole step (two half-steps) and are often illustrating joy or a ratcheting up a notch of excitement. This one is only a slight difference in pitch level, and thus Sting's voice does not sound that much higher. It illustrates the speaker's acceptance of the new reality and the change in meaning of the refrain words—from cynicism to emotional truth.

In the figure, I have listed similar musical ideas in vertical columns. The middle section is almost, but not exactly, like another expository refrain (without the title words), which is why it is in the right-hand column. It begins on the same chord and is the same length as those other sections. After the modulation, we sort of start the song over with a new expository refrain (R2), a verse, and a final chorus. The refrains, indicated in the example by R and R', appear in two different forms. The second one could be classified as the more dissonant of the two, and therefore darker. It is this one that "sticks"; that is to say it is the darker refrain (R') that the song ends with.

The most telling line in this song happens in this last expository refrain: "We try to do the best within the given time." On the surface, the narrator is referring to fatherhood in a broken marriage. He does the best he can in brief visits with his children. (There is also the implication that we try to eat our ice cream before it melts.) It also resonates with the time span of our lives in the larger picture. This is the nature of most healthy adults: just trying to make life the best it can be while we are still alive.

This song works on yet another metaphorical level. Just as it seems to be, at first glance, a simple country song, deeper analysis reveals it to be quite complex. This I believe relates to the dynamics in a family with divorced parents. From the outside, one can simply say: "Oh, they're divorced," but it is always more complicated than that. Relationships between family members become different, and in this song the various chorus and verse forms change over the course of the song. The second expository refrain (set in the park, in the new key) solves the "problem" of the song's formal structure. By returning to the opening chord progression, the song seems to make sense again. As the narrator realizes in the middle section: "It's all connected."

This highlight of *Mercury Falling* is followed by another rather middling song, "All Four Seasons." It is a cute song, dedicated to Sting's daughter Coco (born in 1990),[33] who at the time was five or six. Again the Memphis Horns are employed, and they figure more into the mix than in "You Still Touch Me." Sting relates his daughter's mercurial behavior to unpredictable weather patterns. Wisely, however, it could be applied to any woman, since Sting does not specify the age of the subject.[34]

What is notable about this song's structure is that is seems to have two middle sections. The first middle comes after two verse-refrain pairs. Then after another verse-refrain we get a second middle, starting with the line "Watching the weatherman's been no good at all." Another possible interpretation is that it is an altered verse, because it does in fact end with another refrain. The first middle then comes back before a final verse-refrain.

Another Sting-Dominic Miller collaboration follows: the Brazilian-inspired "La Belle Dame Sans Regrets." This moody song is in faux-French, with a nod to John Keats' poem "La Belle Dame Sans Merci" ("The merciless beautiful woman"). Although the text is largely present for its sonic quality and not its meaning,[35] Sting has claimed that it is "about [his] reaction to the French nuclear tests."[36] In this light "La Belle Dame" could be thought as a personification of France, testing these dangerous weapons "without regrets." Sting had used French before, in "Hungry for You," and will again, in "Perfect Love . . . Gone Wrong."

The song's structure is relatively simple, with two verse-chorus pairs that use approximately the same chord pattern for each. In the middle Kirkland takes a piano solo, one of his few on the album. The last chorus is extended a bit, and after a pause we have a very "cool" coda, with Sting reprising some lines from the song and Colaiuta and Kirkland channeling the clubs of Rio de Janeiro. The influence of Brazilian recording artists like Milton Nascimento and João Gilberto is all over this track.

"Valparaiso" is another neo-folk song, a la "Fields of Gold." This one is just the briefest of sketches, telling of the love of a sailor for his companion back home. The song was written for the soundtrack to Ridley Scott's film *White Squall*.[37] Valparaiso is a port on the southern coast of Chile and thus is very far away from anywhere else. Sting uses the traditional gender of a ship as female and alternately uses the word "she" to mean the ship or the speaker's lover.

The haunting verse melody never wavers and is harmonized slightly differently the first time we hear it. Kathryn Tickell's small pipes and fiddle introduce the waltz tune over a pedal E, which continues through the first part of the verse. A contrasting middle section follows the second verse, beginning as they often do with a new chord. This narrator cannot stay off the sea, and "every road [he] walked would take me down to the sea." This is why the middle inevitably ends up back on the tonic e minor chord.

Like in the previous song, we end with a "cool" coda, with plenty of room for virtuosity from the band. A bass line that is reminiscent of the coda of "I Burn for You" provides the foundation for Kirkland's organ solo and Colaiuta's subdivisions of the beat. This section also calls to mind the central solo passage of "Children's Crusade," with which it shares a key.

The final track on *Mercury Falling*, "Lithium Sunset," is also the shortest and so feels like a "coda" to the album. That is to say, it does not seem like a song that can stand up on its own. It begins with the same tonic note E as "Valparaiso" ended with. However, we soon learn that this E chord is merely an introductory preparation for the new tonic of A major. We also hear another country-style groove that sets a positive mood for this concluding song. B. J. Cole's pedal steel guitar also contributes to the country feel.

The words are based on the alleged benefits of watching the sunset. Not only is it calming and relaxing, but, according to a "South American shaman," the light from the sunset produces lithium in the brain.[38] Whether this is true or not, sunset is one of the only times that the naked eye can see the planet Mercury. Since it is so close to the sun, it sets (or falls) with the sun. Dusk is also a natural time for falling temperatures, thus relating this line back to the opening of "The Hounds of Winter."

Musically, "Lithium Sunset" is almost too short to make much of an impression. As mentioned, the E major chord is a preparation for the tonic of A major. This chord comes back on the repetition of the line "Into another night," again preparing for the home chord of A. The middle once again starts on the relative minor chord, to describe the speaker's "shattered" past. However, the section eventually winds back to A and the start of the last verse. The very last chord of this middle is a surprising F chord (on the word "heal"), which is new for this song and quite foreign to this key. I am not sure why it is there, other than the possibility that Sting did not want to overuse the E chord as a preparatory chord.

Mercury Falling ends with two alternating bass notes (A and D) that fade away. Cole adds his bittersweet sound to illustrate Sting's somewhat resigned reiterations of "Mercury falling." Sometimes, instead of a D major chord alternating with the tonic A, Cole and Miller play a d *minor* chord, which gives this ending a bit of ambiguity. This is fitting for an album with aging as its main subject. Except for a couple of very strong songs, *Mercury Falling* falls short of the excellent releases we had come to expect from this seasoned musician.

Despite this, and despite mixed and lukewarm reviews from critics,[39] Sting still played around the world to sold-out houses, and the album sold well. Even when Sting was mediocre, he made huge amounts of money. His fame had increased throughout the 1990s, with honorary degrees, Grammy awards, collaborations with pop stars around the world, contributions to several film soundtracks, and repeated benefit concerts for the Rainforest Foundation. During this decade he purchased two more properties in addition to Lake House: a beach house in Malibu and "Il Palagio" in Tuscany, near Arezzo.

Throughout the 1990s and beyond, Sting has never sat still. When he is not writing and recording a new album or touring, he is performing benefit concerts for various charities or creating new songs for soundtracks and other projects. Some of these tracks are negligible and/or hard to find, but others are quite good. It would be wonderful if all of these miscellaneous B-sides and one-off songs were to be collected and released on a single disc.

Some of these projects include writing the "theme song" for his home football club, Newcastle United ("Black and White Army"), creating new songs and adapting old ones for the IMAX films *The Living Sea* and *Dolphins,* writing a song for a Japanese resort commercial ("Take Me to the Sunshine"), and later in 2003, contributing a nineteenth-century-style ballad for the Civil War film *Cold Mountain.* The sheer variety of these projects attest to Sting's adaptability and creativity as a songwriter.

The mid-1990s were the era of the CD single, and many artists were under pressure from their record companies to fill out these naturally short, lower-priced releases with extra songs, remixes, or "B-sides" (a term left over from the 45 RPM format). Sting, for his two albums of the period, released several CD singles, each with two or three extras. The focus of this book is on the major releases, but I would like to mention one song in particular.

"Twenty Five to Midnight" was left off the North American version of *Mercury Falling*. It is a song about a failed musician who leaves town to go on tour and also loses his girlfriend in the process. The best part about it is the music, which combines two of Sting's great loves: 1960s soul and odd time signatures. Colaiuta, in a nod to several tracks of the period, often plays a snare hit on every beat. This disguises the fact that the song is in 7/4 (or alternates measures of four with measures of three). The middle section is a hilarious faux-Latin example of this failed band's music ("The Latino Lovers"). Because the time signature remains in seven, this section perfectly illustrates the awkwardness of the fictional band.

6

Hope and Terror

BRAND NEW DAY

After the mild disappointment of the previous album, *Brand New Day* was a welcome change in direction for his fans. Not only does there seem to be a new aesthetic and energy on this album, but there is also a new sound. A big reason for this was a new collaborator named Mark Eldridge, who goes by the name Kipper. He and Sting met in 1997 while working on the song "Freak the Mighty" for the soundtrack to Peter Chelsom's film *The Mighty*. The two have worked together ever since. Kipper is a multi-instrumentalist, programmer, and producer, and he is familiar with the latest musical technology. His talents proved invaluable to Sting, and his electronica-influenced stamp is all over *Brand New Day* (released in October 1999). This new updated sound helped the album reach No. 9 on the Billboard charts and spawned his first top-20 single since 1994. It also won Sting two Grammy Awards, for Best Pop Album and Best Male Pop Vocal Performance.[1]

Right away in the opening song, "A Thousand Years" (co-written with Kipper), we hear the hugely expanded sound world that this album exemplifies. Kipper's exceptional talent for seamlessly integrating sampled and original sounds is evident here and on almost every track. Kipper is likely a follower of Brian Eno, a producer and composer who is considered by many to be a trailblazer in popular music production. Eno's influential and innovative collaborations of the 1970s and 80s with David Bowie, Talking Heads, and U2 remain touchstones of audio excellence. Known especially for his creation of ambient soundscapes, Eno's influence can be felt on most popular songs of today.

One of Sting's new favorite instruments at this time was the Roland Vg-8 guitar synthesizer, which uses a guitar-like method to control whatever sounds the instrument is connected to, via computer or traditional modular synthesizer. In this first song the sound seems to be some sort of sampled viola or similar Middle-Eastern bowed string instrument. Its mournful sound ascends the minor scale up to scale degree five, where it oscillates between that pitch and the one just below it. One of the fundamental principles common to all types of music is that repetition implies eventual change, and the more times a musical gesture is repeated, the greater the urge to vary it becomes. This main melody that Sting introduces on the Vg-8 continues as a through-line in this song. It receives different harmonic treatments throughout the song but consistently states those two oscillating notes seven times.

Sting and Kipper construct the song so that this fundamental melody can be repeated and it does not "clash" with other musical events. During the chorus ("I still love you . . .") it serves as a countermelody to the longer vocal lines. During the third verse it is still there as Sting's vocals provide yet another melodic idea against it. The last chorus is extended and slowed down before it arrives back at the home pitch, coinciding with the return of the oscillating motive.

During this fade-out, one can hear some of Kipper's Eno-influenced "ambient" touches. There are a couple of chirp-like electronic sounds, one in the left channel and one in the right. They are considered ambient sounds because they are not what would be traditionally called "musical" sounds. Oftentimes ambient sounds either do not have a definable pitch or they use microtonal pitches. Microtones are pitches that sound "out of tune": They exist in between the frequencies created by a half-step. As an illustration, a microtonal note could be thought of as played by an imaginary key between two consecutive keys on a piano. It is "out of tune," but it is deliberately so. These pitches serve to enhance the sound world and expand the musical color palette of a song.

"A Thousand Years" makes a great opener for this album, by presenting its major themes of history (both personal and global), time, honesty, and love. It is at its heart a love song, but one in which the speaker situates himself as just one of the six billion people on the planet. In verse one, he is one of a thousand; in verse two, one of a million; in verse three he is "numberless." Despite being just one of many, the fact remains that he loves whomever he is singing to. There is also a touch of the sacred in lines like "I've kept this single faith, I have but one belief." This song is timely, as it was written during the lead-up to 2000, and religious topics were being bandied about because of that significant milestone of the Christian calendar.

"Desert Rose" climbed up the Billboard charts to No. 17, helped by Sting's agreement with Jaguar automobiles for the track's use in its television commercials. But it is a compelling track in its own right. Kipper's production and programming, coupled with guest Algerian *rai* star Cheb Mami, give this song its irresistible Middle-Eastern flavor. Mami's vocal lines pair with Sting's perfectly, and according to him, "matched the gait of the melody as perfectly as a horse and rider."[2]

Sting says that the subject matter grew out of the music this time,[3] and not the other way around as is often the case. It is a generalized first-person point of view that inhabits the "I" of the lyric. Not many details are given about this person, but none are needed. It is about longing for rain in the desert, which suggests a longing for love, for sexual satisfaction. North Africa has a very hot and dry climate, and water is precious and scarce. It is only natural that Sting would incorporate music from this part of the world for a song set in the desert.

The imagery and the song structure seem to be jumbled around in the speaker's mind. Sting has said that an element of his songwriting process is free association with an initial idea,[4] and in "Desert Rose" the central image is of a flower in the desert. The flower, because it needs water to survive, represents the presence of water and thus the ideas of thirst (and hunger) and satisfaction, temptation and self-control, and ultimately, sin and the biblical Fall. The rose itself has been used countless times as a symbol of temptation, with its beauty and wonderful aroma coupled with thorns that can hurt if grasped. Sting addresses each of these qualities at various points in the song.

As mentioned above, the ideas are all jumbled together and seem to swirl about, creating a rather complex song structure. This is also related to the "dreaming" of the speaker. So the first four lines (the first verse) in English return twice, almost becoming as important as the chorus itself ("This desert rose . . ."). The second chorus comes after a pair of verses (verse three and the return of verse one) and uses new text over the chorus chords. To add to the confusion, this chorus begins with the opening line of the first verse ("I dream of rain . . ."). After a middle section that recalls the introduction featuring Mami by himself, we have a further return of verse one, followed by two choruses, the second of which is also altered.

This final chorus, which refers back to the second chorus's mention of perfume, addresses the biblical idea of temptation. The "memory of Eden" calls to mind the story of the forbidden fruit that Eve took from the Tree of Knowledge. Thus the last word of Sting's lyric could simply refer to autumn, but more likely it refers to both the season and the "Fall of Man" and the idea of original sin.

Cheb Mami's voice is the first we hear, and he wrote the Arabic words for his part.[5] His words also speak of desire and pure love of one thing, either human or divine.[6] He sings verse one by himself, also during the middle section after the second chorus, and then joins Sting for the last verse and choruses. His amazing technique and high-pitched voice weave in and out of Sting's song to great effect. He is sometimes doubled by a group of string players, conducted and arranged by Farhat Bouallagui and probably recorded in Paris. They also play during the instrumental break just before the return of verse one. The song ends as it began: with the mystery and romance of this "postcard" view of the Middle East receding into the distance like a mirage.

The next song, "Big Lie Small World," transitions smoothly from "Desert Rose" by beginning with the same chord tone (C). However, the home "tonic" chord happens on the next chord (E minor 9). This is another one of Sting's unusual time-signature experiments (of which there are a couple on *Brand New Day*). It is similar to "I Hung My Head" in that it is 9/8 divided 2+3+2+2 (although the way the nine eighth notes are grouped varies quite a bit). It is slower than the earlier song but was still probably composed on the guitar. This time, however, the chords are plucked with multiple fingers rather than "picked" with one note per finger (creating a "broken chord" idea).

"Big Lie Small World" is another "narrative song," written in 13 quatrains with brief refrains in three places. It also has much in common with other of Sting's "love-triangle" songs, especially "Seven Days," with its somewhat meek protagonist and a burly other man. This time, however, the guy gets caught. He sends a letter to his ex-lover, lying to her and himself that he feels better now. He has second thoughts after mailing it and sets off across town to retrieve it before it arrives. He winds up feeling so desperate and frightened when he sees the boyfriend and the postman that he hits them both, grabs the letter, and flees. This rather extreme reaction makes for a somewhat unbelievable scenario, but Sting makes a great song out of it nonetheless.

The main point of the song, after all, is humor, and the music reflects that. The 9/8 time signature in "I Hung My Head" was described by Sting as "loping" and for him called to mind a horse dragging a body.[7] Here, the main image is not so morbid, but the rhythm still implies a sense of awkwardness and stumbling. The protagonist here is certainly not the most confident of people, and by the end we realize that he is either in custody or at least about to go to court. We can also assume that his love interest was none too impressed by his actions.

The way the music illustrates the bumbling of the main character is through the addition of chords that seem to compound the problems that he creates. The home (tonic) chord, as mentioned above, is E minor. This is also the only chord that makes up the refrain of "Big Lie Small World," when the speaker acknowledges the truth and his bad luck. So this E minor chord could represent the truth or the final outcome of the speaker's fortunes. Each verse begins on a C chord, which could be heard as him trying to "fix" things: writing the letter, which was a big lie, trying to retrieve the letter, assaulting the postman and the boyfriend, and running away with the letter. But each time, he ends up back at the "truth," or E minor.

The first couple of verses, and the first one after each chorus, use just two chords (C major 7 and e minor), but as more verses happen and the man tries new ways of getting out of the situation, more chords are added to the mix. In verses 4, 7, the middle (which covers quatrains 8 and 9), 12, and 13, the e minor home chord is not even sounded. So the speaker, in a sense, strays ever further from the truth, just as the music veers away from the tonic.

The middle section (stanzas 8 and 9) is at a perfect spot in the song: It tells of where the woman is staying, in an "opulent" flat or house. Thus it is introduced musically in the relative major key (G). Also, Sting's vocal phrasing differs here from the rest of the song. In quatrain eight, the second and third lines are sung together without a break. While the speaker sits and waits for the postman, we get a wordless refrain that highlights Chris Botti's trumpet playing.[8]

As the climax and denouement of Sting's little tragicomedy plays out, the chords become more chromatic and dissonant against the tonic chord. In the last verse (stanza 13), the last line of wishing to fly away is harmonized with a B♭ chord, or as far away as harmonically possible from E minor. Of course, our sad little man must resign himself to his fate with a mournful trumpet solo by Botti that leads into the next scene.

We are back in North Africa, it seems, judging by the *darbouka* (played by Ettamri Mustapha) and traditional "Eastern"-flavored sound, for a story that could be inspired by the *Arabian Nights*. In "After the Rain Has Fallen," a thief breaks into a princess's chamber, intending to steal jewels and money, and ends up sleeping with her instead (or, possibly, raping her). The woman makes the fateful decision to leave her world and her arranged marriage and run off with the thief. Whether they do or not is unclear, but the liberating music suggests so.

The conceit of the *Arabian Nights* stories is that, in order to save her own life, Scheherazade must tell the evil sultan a new story every night; otherwise she will be killed like all the previous women. So Scheherazade never finishes her stories in one night; she leaves the sultan hanging every night to stay alive. Sting might be using this same survival technique in this song. By not supplying a clear-cut ending to the story, he is leaving us hungry for more. This also explains why "After the Rain Has Fallen" ends on an inconclusive chord.

This song is another one that has two main musical ideas: the verses and the chorus. After we hear this song, the chorus is really what we remember most; I think this is what Sting intended. The main point of the song, ultimately, is that love is eternal. After all our worldly concerns and physical items have been lost, what remains (in a healthy individual) is love. This is the argument that the thief (via Sting) is making.

The five verses, then, are just setup. The entire second half of the song is made up of the chorus and the middle, in which the princess entreats the thief to steal her away and take her out of her situation. And, true to form, Sting does this musically by changing key (using his favorite "hidden modulation" technique) up a minor third. The last two choruses are some of the most enthralling of Sting's solo career. Not only is excitement created by the pitch level moving up, but the line "still be love in the world" is sung in counterpoint with the existing chorus melody. Pure pop magic.

The inconclusive ending is given an "inner groove" sound (a looped sample of a scratchy record) to transition to the much more sedate and domestic "Perfect Love . . . Gone Wrong." This song is a great example of the author/speaker tension that is present in some songs. In short, the speaker here is a dog, who feels jealous and slighted by the new "roommate": his owner's new boyfriend. Sting wanted to have the song exist in two languages so that it mimics, for non-French speakers anyway, the dog's experience when being chastised by the woman. Sting also presents the French rap sections (performed by French rapper Sté) in a different key than the verses—this sets them apart harmonically in addition to the texture change to a hip-hop groove. Although "key" is not a crucial element in most rap music, in these sections, the bass line alternates between the notes D♭ and E♭, in a pattern reminiscent of "Be Still My Beating Heart." This upper note (E♭) is eventually used as the tonic for the final choruses.

These final choruses, similar to "After the Rain Has Fallen," make up most of the second half of the song. They also include the verse melody of the words "He won't love you like I love you" as a countermelody. For the second-to-last chorus (before the beginning of the fade), Sting sings a "coda verse" over the chorus, plus the verse melody. This concatenation of three melodic ideas is a wonderful example of counterpoint in popular music. Sting introduces each musical idea separately: in the first verse (with the Vg-8) and the second verse (in the vocal), in the chorus ("To have found this perfect life"), and finally in the "coda verse." The combination of all three of these ideas is quite complex rhythmically and melodically, but we as listeners can comprehend it because of the careful way in which each idea was introduced.

Sting's sense of humor and skill with wordplay is evident in the lyrics. His very clever rhymes really capture the mindset of the dog who feels he is being replaced. We can only imagine how the dog, who thought he and his owner had a "perfect love," and the boyfriend get along. In a word, not well. The French rap, as stated earlier, represents the owner talking to the dog in a scolding tone of voice (she can initially be heard during the introduction, answering the telephone—presumably talking to her boyfriend).[9] One can fairly easily get the gist of what she is saying, even without a translation: "You'll just have to get used to him," "I need a man, not a dog, for a boyfriend," and "If you don't start behaving, I will have to get rid of you."

The "fade-out" chorus includes a return to the verse's bass riff while the backing vocals continue the chorus, and Sté recalls some lines from her rap. We leave the scene with the central problem still unresolved: that of the dog and boyfriend not liking each other. The change of key to match the rap sections might imply some sort of resolution, but this is counteracted by the recall of the verse's bass line. This points to the dog remaining obstinate despite the woman's entreaties and leaves the song delightfully ambiguous in its ending.

In "Perfect Love . . . Gone Wrong," Sting successfully places himself as author in the mind of a dog and alternately identifies with the woman (voiced by Sté). The next song, "Tomorrow We'll See," continues this speaker/author separation by telling a story from the perspective of a male transvestite prostitute. This song resonates with others of his body of work that involve "the seedy parts of town": "Roxanne" and "Low Life." As Sting writes in his introduction to the song in *Lyrics,* these men put their lives at risk for what they do.[10] He does not judge them, as the speaker encourages the listeners not to do. Sting learned about them through his wife Styler's documentary film *Boys from Brazil,* which she produced for the BBC in 1993.

This little sketch of one prostitute just gives a snapshot of what their life is like: nocturnal, secret, dangerous, and tragic. The most telling and sad lines in the song are the middle: "And no, it's not in my plan / for someone to care who I am." This is in a way a tragic answer to the unresolved story behind "Roxanne." Because of the morals of a given society, some people are perceived as less important than others, and so no one cares when one of these "undesirables" dies or is killed.

A string orchestra, arranged and conducted by Dave Hartley, ushers us into this nocturnal world of back alleys and loading docks, calling to mind a soundtrack to a 1950s spy movie. Branford Marsalis returns briefly to the Sting fold and provides a classy clarinet solo. The whole atmosphere is reminiscent of George Gershwin's "Summertime," which is apt, as that is a very ironic song about the lower classes on the margins of society.

The structure of "Tomorrow We'll See" is typical, with a heavy reliance on verses (there are four in a row before we get the first chorus), a return of the string introduction after the clarinet solo, and the transitioning middle section mentioned earlier. After this the music moves up a step, and we get the final verse and chorus pair in the new key. This modulation, rather than uplifting, seems to simply confirm and heighten the sad state of affairs for these men. We are left to ponder what tomorrow will bring.

Next, on the North American version of the CD, we only get the first 19 seconds of "The End of the Game." The reasons for this further omission (one track was left off of the North American versions of the two previous albums as well) are unknown, but it is extremely annoying. On *Brand New Day,* it seems like a cheap trick to list 10 tracks on the back of the case when there are really only 9. I hope that this disc, along with *Ten Summoner's Tales* and *Mercury Falling,* will eventually be reissued in North America with all of the songs that Sting intended them to have. "The End of the Game" is a perfectly good and catchy song, but probably not many Sting fans in North America have heard it.

This brief, initially mysterious interlude is followed by, "Fill Her Up," a wonderful song about envy, temptation, crime, guilt, and epiphany. It features James Taylor as a guest vocalist, singing the part of the "big shot." It also features the welcome return of pedal steel player B. J. Cole, who added so much to the "country" tracks on *Mercury Falling*. "Fill Her Up" is a curious hybrid of a country groove, with a second part of gospel in 7/8. I am not aware of any gospel songs in asymmetrical time signatures, but put through the Sting songwriting filter, it makes sense. The original version of this song was entirely in 7/8.[11] By breaking the song in two, it is far more effective at expressing the change of heart and epiphany of the speaker.

The first section, the "country" song, uses characteristic, almost cliché techniques and details of the style. Sting as bass player is in "two to a bar" mode (which he loves to do), common to country and bluegrass. Cole's pedal steel, Miller's twangy electric, and James Taylor's shouted interjections all add up to the dusty gas station scene. The "big shot" inspires in our protagonist an ill-advised scheme of stealing money from his boss to head to Las Vegas, get married, and live it up. It is an age-old story: Young person sees older person with money, flashy things, and success and presumes him to be happy because of his success. The message of the song, and Sting's message to us, is that happiness cannot be bought—it must be created, and it takes hard work and time. The "voice" that our character hears in the forest glade during his epiphany tells him to "fill up" his girlfriend with love and good things, that this is the best way to have a rich life.

The choruses ("I'm gonna take my baby one day") start on a chord just below the tonic of A, for a little variety and to act as a signal that this is a new section. After the second chorus is when the speaker stops and feels the cold money in his hands. Appropriately, the second chorus stops on an intermediate chord, not returning to A but beginning the synthesized-choir transition to the 7/8 gospel section. When the gospel choir enters from a long way off, they are softly using the same progression as the earlier chorus.[12] As they build and grow closer to the speaker, he eventually joins the chorus, but he is now talking to himself. One can almost see the young man running home to his girlfriend with this newfound love for life.

This is quite a song and quite a statement from someone who has probably been in the same situation himself, coming as he did from a working-class upbringing, pursuing the glamorous life of an international pop star, and maturing gracefully over time. I think that Sting, with all of his success and riches, has learned that what really matters in life is being happy. The coda of this song is a document of Sting at his happiest: jamming with his friends in 7/8. This is his heaven.

The next track, "Ghost Story," seems like a throwback to the *Mercury Falling*-era folk- and country-influenced sound. Also, the subject matter is dark at first and concerns regret, death, and lost love. Still, it serves as a good foil for the rest of the techno- and electronica-heavy album. And it exhibits the same high level of craftsmanship that one would expect from Sting.

The narrator exemplifies many Northern European and American middle-aged men, who rarely express their feelings openly. This man has been telling himself that he does not miss his wife (presumed to be dead). This is the "ghost" of the title. This is not a "ghost story" in the traditional sense. It is more about feeling the presence of a loved one after they have died. The song is framed by the sun setting at the outset and the moon sinking at the end: Thus the man has been thinking and pondering all night. The words also make several references to a trial, using courtroom language such as "case," "jury," and "prosecution." Perhaps this man was a lawyer/solicitor? In any case, in the first half of the song, he tries to use logic and rationality to explain away his feelings of apathy about his wife's death.[13]

In the middle section (beginning "What is the force that binds the stars?"), the longer lines and change in rhyme scheme from abcb to aabb indicate a change in musical setting (which is what happens, as will be discussed below). These stanzas alternate lines about the mystery of creation and how the universe stays together without our interference. The speaker realizes that not everything is under his control, and some things just are and cannot be completely explained by science or rational thought. In the final section, he connects this realization with his love for his wife. The last stanza contains the same aabb rhyme scheme as the middle, further illustrating its connection to the cosmic truth that the speaker discovers.

"Ghost Story" has always been tricky for me to hear rhythmically. The rhythmic "key" that only gets clarified in the last couple of verses is that all of the verse melody notes happen on the "off-beats." In Miller's guitar introduction, the downbeats are always the lower pitches. Until that last section of the song, I have the habit of hearing the off-beats as downbeats and vice versa. This phenomenon is perhaps best called "rhythmic disorientation"; the opposite of what John Miller Chernoff terms "rhythmic orientation."[14] Whatever terminology one chooses would explain that once the country groove finally starts (at 3:32), the pulse becomes crystal clear.

This I think represents the speaker's clarity in his own mind at this point in the song, right after the middle section. Suddenly the previously confusing rhythm makes sense and can be put in the correct rhythmic context. Similarly, in his realization that he was wearing a "mask" to protect himself, and his new recognition of his place in the universe, the melodic-rhythmic orientation becomes resolved. Moreover, Sting uses another of his "hidden modulations" to express this new reality. Similarly to "I'm So Happy I Can't Stop Crying," the middle section is used as the transformative moment, and the remainder of the song happens in a higher key (in this case, a whole step up).

The closing track is a fittingly exuberant and optimistic finale to this excellent "turn of the century" album. "Brand New Day" equates the starting over in relationships with starting over in time (both with a "new day" and a new century). Sting, especially in the later choruses, uses all sorts of playful metaphors with sexual connotations to represent the idea (from a particularly male perspective) of restarting (i.e., "I'm a flagpole to your nation").

This is another song in which the second half is almost entirely made up of the chorus. In this case, however, it is hard to differentiate between "chorus" and "verse," since the two have such similar chord progressions. The chorus, for this song's purposes, is purely defined by the text (which begins with "Turn the clock to zero . . ."). The verses come in two incarnations: one for verses one and two and another, more elaborated version for verses three and four. The first one is also the progression of the first chorus and for all sections in the last half of the song, including the harmonica solo by guest Stevie Wonder. Since the chord pattern stays the same, it puts more of an emphasis on the melody and text. This makes the "millennial" chorus ("Stand up") more prominent and literally "choral" in nature: Sting wants the whole world to sing along. The collective, inclusive use of the term "lovers" is both sexual and spiritual and connects to his ideas about universal love (which will be explored on his album *Sacred Love*). It is a song about renewal and personal rejuvenation, which is fitting because that is exactly what *Brand New Day* represented in Sting's career.

The humorous sexual metaphors continue under reiterations of the title as well as "Stand up!" As this fades, the mood darkens and Kipper's ambient sounds return to the fore, with a thought-provoking recall of the opening track "A Thousand Years." This reference ties in with the theme of "restarting" of the song, but it also implies a cyclical interpretation of the album as a whole. In most Western schools of thought, time is conceived of as linear. Hence the idea of a timeline and even our consecutively numbered calendar system are linear concepts. Many other societies, both ancient and modern, have a cyclical or circular conception of time, where events repeat themselves over time, much like the seasons. Sting, by ending his millennial album with a cyclic recall of the first track (which had to do with time itself), is suggesting that perhaps we as twenty-first-century people might know our world (and ourselves) better if we learn to think of time as more circular rather than linear.

. . . *ALL THIS TIME*

Sting hit the road once again, with a somewhat expanded band lineup, including Kipper, Katché, pianist Jason Rebello, and Botti.[15] The tour took them all over the world once again and ended up in London in July 2001. It was one of his most successful tours ever and proved that here was a recording artist with staying power.

. . . *All This Time* was the live CD and DVD record of this tour, although the backing band was really assembled in order to record the performance at Il Palagio, Sting's estate in Italy. The performance was only for about 150 invited guests and VIPs. On many of the tracks, he expands and alters the arrangements to allow room for solos by Chris Botti, Rebello, and others, much like he did on *Bring on the Night*. The CD charted at No. 32 in the United States.

Some highlights of the performance include a soul-infused, minor-key version of "All This Time," a newly expanded version of "Fragile" (which was released as a single), a quieter, moody take on "Don't Stand So Close to Me" (similar to the version on the 2007–8 reunion tour set list), and Sting's new words to "Dienda" by Kenny Kirkland, who passed away in 1998.

A notable fact regarding this performance is that it happened on September 11, 2001, approximately six hours after the terrorist attacks on the United States. The DVD includes documentary footage of the rehearsals from the preceding week. The day of the performance, after hearing about the attacks, we see the band going back and forth between going ahead with the performance and canceling it outright. The entire performance was supposed to have been broadcast live over the Internet, but in the event they decided to do only "Fragile" for the live feed. This was an appropriate choice and involved a last-minute set list change to feature this song about the futility of violence on that dark day. Significantly, "Desert Rose," featuring Cheb Mami, was cut from the final concert; as the world was learning about who was behind the attacks, Mami (a Muslim) quietly left Sting's villa. A wonderful performance of "Desert Rose" during the previous day's rehearsal is included on the DVD.

The documentary portion of the DVD feels like what *Bring on the Night* was supposed to be but wasn't. It includes real, insightful (not staged) comments from Sting and others about songwriting, rehearsing, and being a working musician. Especially during the conversation about what to do following the terrorist attacks, these musicians' humanity and sensitivity shines through. As Janice Pendarvis says: "I *need* to sing about this." The concert ends up being a testament to the power of music to work through our collective grief that comes from tragedies such as this.

Sacred Love

Sting's most recent album as of this writing is 2003's *Sacred Love* (released in October of that year). He mentions that it was written and recorded during the run-up to the U.S.–led invasion of Iraq, and that the optimism of *Brand New Day* was hard to maintain.[16] It seemed that the words of "History Will Teach Us Nothing" were all too prescient. There is an undercurrent of anger and protest on this album, which is a welcome subject matter for the sometimes complacent Sting. Unfortunately, however, these emotions and views on the Iraq War only rarely seem to come to the surface musically.

In many ways, *Sacred Love* is a logical step forward in Sting's interest in electronic and dance music that was introduced on *Brand New Day*. Kipper, the musician largely responsible for this expansion of Sting's sound, returns here as a collaborator. A few of the tracks feature special guests, such as Mary J. Blige on "Whenever I Say Your Name" and sitarist Anoushka Shankar on "The Book of My Life." This album went to No. 3 on the Billboard chart but did not produce a successful single by Sting's standards. He essentially used the same band as for . . . *All This Time*.

On the whole, *Sacred Love* seems to suffer from a lack of creativity in both songwriting and the overall sound of the album. There are too many songs that have a similar vibe, thus producing a rather mono-textured disc. Not too many of the tracks are particularly memorable in the way that previous songs are.

The opening track, "Inside," is an example of a slightly missed opportunity. The aforementioned anger is there, and in fact it can get quite scary, but it just does not seem to go far enough to really make its points effectively. The basic premise or conflict is interesting: an inside/outside duality and tension, where we witness a man breaking out of himself, and we simultaneously go deeper inside his soul. And it is a frightening place. This is the inner journey of someone who has been hurt by love and is angry at it. There is no real resolution here, just a nightmarish vision of a staircase up to the sky, ending with a swirling, frustrated coda.

This is another one of Sting's "list" songs, with various forms of the list idea in each section. In the verses, every line starts with either the words "inside" or "outside." The chorus lines all start with "love," and the coda uses command forms of "love me" and various other verbs. Sting is imitating the innermost thoughts of this person and how confused and angry they are. It is an interesting idea, and one that has resonances back to "Synchronicity II," with its window into the soul of the monster inside the suburban family man. That song, however, had a definite goal and climax, with the monster arriving at the cottage door and surfacing in the man. Here the goal just seems to be almost random wordplay with "-ate" verbs. "Replicate me" is the last command verb in the text, and it is unclear what that has to do with anger and a broken-hearted speaker.

The music is very dark and multi-layered, which reflects the troubled state of mind. A slow ascending guitar pattern, reminiscent of "Mad about You," is the main riff of the song and is associated with the "Inside" stanzas. Almost the opposite musical idea (a descending pattern) is used for lines that begin with "outside." The chorus ("Love is the child of an endless war. . .") is the only moment of relief in this unrelentingly minor-mode song. It briefly uses the relative major key of C before returning to the home key of a minor.

After the second chorus, the music modulates up a step for the crucial stanza of climbing the staircase. The problem is that the texture at this point is so thick that it is hard to discern the words. This may also be because these lines are sung with much longer, stretched-out note values—we are not used to listening at that level of rhythm in the context of this song.

Next comes an interesting stanza: The narrator is now "thrown" into the sky and, through his breathless exhortations, seems to progress from the love of a baby to that of a dying man in about 20 seconds. It is almost like the speaker's life is flashing before his eyes, except that this is not a joyful recollection. It sounds like, in his almost shouted, rap-like vocal delivery, this man had not been loved much in his life and the anger is now boiling over. This ties in with some of the chorus lines "defining" love as all sorts of things that it is traditionally not.

The ending guitar pattern is quite dissonant and seems to cycle around as the "spiral staircase" does. It mimics the "outside" pattern, but it is not the same as in the old key (i.e., it is not simply transposed). Also, the circular string melody floats overhead. During these last stanzas, Sting seems to be rushing to pack all of these verbs in. One is unsure why. Perhaps because the speaker is "falling" into the sky? Underneath Sting's voice and Miller's guitar, everything else gets sort of sucked out of the mix, which represents the "going inside" idea. But for me, the ending sort of peters out. One rarely gets the sense that Sting is not sure how to end a song, but that may have happened here.

The opening of "Send Your Love," the second track on the album, paraphrases the well-known stanza:

> To see a World in a Grain of Sand,
> And a Heaven in a Wild Flower,
> Hold Infinity in the palm of your hand,
> And Eternity in an hour. (William Blake, "Auguries of Innocence")

The reason Sting includes this idea, as he says in his introduction to the song in *Lyrics,* is that he shares Blake's mistrust of organized religion and believes that the world needs to find the answers beyond religion.[17] His use of the idea of finding the sacred in the smallest example of nature that is visible (a grain of sand) speaks to his focus on seeing some sort of divinity in everyday life. So the philosophy behind the song is to conceive of love as a religion and to ensure the continuity of the planet by "sending" love into the future—through our children, by our actions, in our hope. Sting has said: "I think the world is made better incrementally by small gestures . . . Equally, you can make the world a negative place . . . by small acts of meanness and greed and unkindness. So I believe we are responsible for making the world."[18]

What Sting is espousing is very similar to the ideas of the Unitarian Universalist Church. Some of their members are committed atheists, and some are theists, but they do share the belief that only humanity can save itself, and that in order to do so we must think beyond religion or conceive of all religions as one big religion. This is also the belief of many left-leaning Christians. As Sting sings: "There's no religion that's right or winning."

"Send Your Love," for all its heavy and philosophical subject matter, is essentially a dance track. Thus, Sting wisely keeps the harmony relatively simple and instead focuses on the rhythm and vocal delivery. We open with the flamenco guitar of Vicente Amigo, who plays a short introduction in e minor before the main key of a minor arrives. The Blake paraphrase serves as a kind of "introductory verse," sung slower than all succeeding verses and including the lowest note (a low A) that Sting sings on record. After a brief chorus, we hear the characteristic Mediterranean-flavored "brass" melody, most likely sampled. The next verse ("Inside your mind is a relay station") really gets the dance element going. Sting's vocal delivery is now twice as fast as the first verse, and it propels the groove nicely.

The song has a simple structure, with the only "break" happening after the second chorus in the sampled "brass" melody. In the third verse, Sting "fills out" the bass line by moving down stepwise a couple of times instead of staying on the note A. The coda has a bit of Amigo playing, but he seems quite underused here.

The one unqualified commercial success from *Sacred Love* was "Whenever I Say Your Name," a duet with R&B artist Mary J. Blige. In early 2004, this song won the Grammy Award for Best Pop Collaboration with Vocals. Sting has called Blige "the heir apparent to Aretha Franklin,"[19] and she does share some traits with that formidable voice.

The words use one of Sting's favorite combinations of romantic and spiritual love (see "Sacred Love"). In fact, this song could possibly be viewed as either about a love interest or purely as a meditation on God. The incantation of the name of a deity is the quickest way for the believer to enter into a prayerful state. A name can also be used as a mantra in Eastern-style meditation; the repetition of it allows the seeker to shut out all other thoughts. This song is a type of meditation, in a popular music context. The "mantra," if you will, is the repetition of "whenever." That word begins almost every line.

This incredibly harmonically complex song allegedly has a direct borrowing from a Bach keyboard prelude, but Sting does not recollect which one.[20] In any case, the first chorus exhibits a very Bach-like sequence that generally moves from C major to a minor. The verses also confirm that key as the "tonic," but no chord is held for very long until the coda. The second chorus, very sneakily, is actually sung a third lower than the first (i.e., in A major), but we don't notice it because it still feels like a "brightening" of the previous verse key of a minor. This chorus, which includes text from verses one and two, moves from A major to E minor/major, which is the key of the funky coda.

The end of this chorus, in a classical, Bach-like context, would be called a "half-cadence." The guitar arpeggios seem to float down like snowflakes over a sustained E. In the classical world, this held chord would build an expectation to eventually move to the tonic of A. But here, the coda simply (and almost subversively) stays on that same bass note. I believe that Sting intended this ending to sound "endless" and "eternal"; thus sounding the home chord again would have sounded too neat and tidy. This infinite feeling ties back to the text, with its spiritual and romantic themes of love and praying "that day will last forever."

The initial guitar arpeggio chimes in every four measures, connecting back to the falling chord section. E minor/major was probably chosen ahead of time as the chord that the song should end with. It happens to be a good key for both Sting and Blige to sing in. Sting also throws in a reference to "We'll Be Together" from 16 years earlier. It continues the motif of this "back and forth" duet, rather than a melody-harmony type of duet (a la Simon & Garfunkel).

The next song is problematic and seems to contradict Sting's earlier claim that, for him, "There's no religion . . ." "Dead Man's Rope" has a quite strong Christian message, despite his explanation that the title is another name for *ayahuasca,* the vegetal tea drink that Sting was introduced to in 1987 in Brazil.[21] This naturally occurring hallucinogenic substance has been used for centuries by Brazilians of all stripes for revelatory and soul-searching purposes. There are even churches that use it regularly as part of their worship practices.

Still, if one did not know the nickname for this substance, one would interpret this song as a religious conversion story. "Dead Man's Rope" happens in two distinct halves: The first half ends with the second middle section ("I'm just hanging here in space"). This middle is, so far, the most active music we have had: It is reflecting the "wandering" of the speaker. It ends by literally "hanging" in the space of a G chord, and one could imagine a simpler song ending here.

The music, however, signals a mysterious change in direction and repeats the middle section a step up (another "hidden modulation"). An angel leads the speaker into this new key, and we end this middle section with a sly reference to 1983's "Walking in Your Footsteps," except in a very Christian context. After that, the resolution of the converted man's problems is represented by sounding the chorus up a step from the original (in D major), and changing "walk away in . . ." to "walk away *from* . . ." The rain of the first half of the song changes from a suicidal, depressed image to one of healing and forgiveness.

"Never Coming Home" is another dance track, this time featuring pianist Jason Rebello. The story is of a wife who leaves her husband for unspecified reasons. It can thus be categorized as one of Sting's "divorce songs," along with "I'm So Happy I Can't Stop Crying." It also represents a new take on the "love-triangle song." Sting uses all three points of view in the lyric: first, second, and third person. The "you" of the first three verses refers to the woman, the next two verses are third person, describing the woman on the train, and last verses are in the voice of the husband. Each chorus uses these three points of view to say the same thing: that there were too many broken promises from the husband, and she leaves a good-bye letter to him. Sting only needs change a few pronouns and tenses to make this work.

The situation described in this song is reminiscent of The Beatles' "She's Leaving Home," and that song may have been in the back of Sting's mind while writing this one. However, The Beatles track uses the young girl who runs away as a metaphor for the generation gap, coming out as it did in the "Summer of Love" of 1967. "Never Coming Home" is thus a song of a mature artist, who knows that sometimes not all is well in a seemingly happy marriage.

If "Inside" felt like a reworking of "Mad about You," then this track sounds like a dance mix of "Fragile." The guitar riff is nearly identical, and the verse melody works in similar ways. I do not think that this is a deliberate reference to the earlier song, since thematically they have very little to do with one another. There is a possibility that this couple represents Sting's parents, who divorced after he moved away from home. Sting witnessed his mother having an affair with the man that she eventually married, and this episode has haunted him all his life. He is at least familiar with this type of failed marriage.[22]

Unlike "She's Leaving Home," the key stays the same throughout the song, which makes metaphoric sense, as the woman has made up her mind to leave before the song starts. The music, however, in my opinion does not reflect the story or the three different perspectives very well. It is a fun dance number, but what does club music have to do with divorce? Does it represent the woman's newfound freedom? The best part of this track is the extended piano solo by Jason Rebello at the end and during the fade. This young British pianist's playing reminded me of Kenny Kirkland, which was confirmed when I learned that Kirkland introduced Rebello to Sting.[23]

A unique point of view is offered by "Stolen Car (Take Me Dancing)." The main narrator is a young car thief who imagines (or psychically senses, as Sting says in *Lyrics*)[24] the lives of the owners of the vehicle. We learn the basics of the husband and wife from the thief, but the choruses are told from the perspective of the husband's mistress. This is a rich family, with two kids who go to private school and a husband who often "works late." The mistress just wants to have at least one night where she doesn't have to hide the affair. She feels trapped in this situation, and we never find out if anything significant happens after the song is over.

Whether the thief is psychic or not, he functions in a literary sense as an omniscient observer. As figure 6.1 shows, he imagines this love triangle and also speaks in the voice of the mistress. In a way, the car thief is taking on the function that Sting usually fulfills as songwriter. At the end of the song, the young man disappears into the night, just as Sting ends the narrative and never discloses what happens next.

The harmonic palette of "Stolen Car" is similar to other "nocturnal" songs of Sting's, such as "Sister Moon," "It's Probably Me," and "Tomorrow We'll See." This is partially due to the "added tones" in all three of these minor-key songs and the heavy synth-string sound that they share. This song starts out in g minor and uses a pretty standard structure of verse-chorus alternation, although there are only three verses. The middle section functions as the transition to the new key of e minor, a minor third down from the beginning. This "key relationship" (moving down in key instead of up) is also found, on this album, in "Whenever I Say Your Name" and, as we shall see, at the

Figure 6.1
Schematic of Points-of-View in "Stolen Car (Take Me Dancing)"

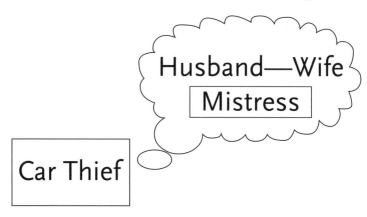

end of "The Book of My Life." An earlier song that does this is "The Soul Cages." It has the effect of "gravitas"—becoming more serious instead of an elevation of mood. Sting also wants us to know that at the end of the song we are in a different place from where we started, but with the qualifier that it is not necessarily a happier place. In "Stolen Car," he uses this new key to end the song darkly and to underscore the seriousness of the situation and also, mentioned above, to signal the "disappeared" quality of the car, the car thief, and possibly the marriage itself, as well as Sting's resolution of the situation.

"Forget about the Future" is a refreshing moment of levity on this otherwise serious album. For most of the song, it is a funky, mid-tempo swing tune with blues-derived chords. It is basically a foreplay song, where the man at one point compares the couple's history to world history. He is saying, "Let's worry about our problems later and get back to what we know how to do, which is make love." Despite a teasing glimpse of the past, recorded in an "old-time" sort of way, the woman does not give in to the man's demands, at least not in the context of this song.

For the first part of the song, Sting keeps his vocal register low, which resonates with the intimacy of the song. During the third chorus, the last three chords bring us up a half-step for the rest of the song (it ends in E). This provides a nice context for the "acoustic" verse four, which uses a stand-up bass, piano, drums with brushes, and trombone and is "magically" introduced with the strum of a harp. The sound gets squelched down to just the middle frequencies, and the whole band suddenly only comes out of the left speaker (suggesting an old-fashioned "mono" gramophone or radio). This brief interlude is reminiscent of the middle "refined" section of "She's Too Good for Me."

But no, it was just "the merest ghost of the past," and the chorus returns with a summation of all the reasons why the woman does not want to give in. In this respect, it is in the same playful, coquettish category of song as "Heavy Cloud No Rain." Here, though, the coda music suggests that the "mast" really does get raised, and they finally get intimate. We end with an extended brass chorus that bleeds into the next track, "This War."

By far the most topical song on the album, it also gives Miller a chance to shine. "This War" is a straight-ahead rocker, with an easy-to-follow structure of alternating verse-chorus. The influence of Cream and other blues-rock bands of the 1960s and 70s is notable on this track. There are some nice Sting touches, like the wordless high melody that introduces each chorus and the elision that happens at the end of the last verse going into the last chorus. This chorus, instead of the four-bar pattern that characterizes the rest of the song, uses a three-bar pattern so that each stanza seems to happen earlier than we expect. Here, Sting lists all the things that he feels are being attacked (besides terrorism and Iraq): democracy, religion, nature, education, the environment, compassion, and "love and life itself."

As noted earlier, *Sacred Love* was written prior to the U.S. invasion of Iraq, and so the ending line of this song was an entreaty that of course went unheeded. It is very easy to read these lyrics as solely aimed at the administration of George W. Bush (2001–2009), but Sting wisely keeps them general and could be addressing any political leader on the eve of battle. After all, Sting's leader, British Prime Minister Tony Blair, was just as much of a hawk in 2003 as many in the Bush administration were. Unfortunately, just as these lyrics could be applied to several past wartime presidents, they will be applicable to future leaders as well.

The main problem with this track, however, is the recording quality. Earlier, I said that "Inside" was a missed musical opportunity. "This War" is a good song, but the mix is so guitar-heavy that Sting's voice gets lost. Without the words right in front of one, it is hard to understand what he is singing. Perhaps he was simply not in good voice that day, but that kind of problem can usually be compensated for in the studio.

"The Book of My Life" is obviously related to the writing of his memoir, *Broken Music,* which was published in November 2003. Sting mentions in *Lyrics* that he loves to sit by the fire and think.[25] This is a similar setup to the narrator in "Ghost Story." In this new song, Sting (or the speaker) imagines that the embers are the burning pages of his book. He uses the metaphor of the book as representing a life, with "pages," "chapters," and "sentences" (also a pun on a prison sentence). This book in question is also a mystery, because we never know how our "book" (our lives) will end. Ultimately, the song becomes a love song: "And all that's left is you."

This very pretty song features rising star Anoushka Shankar on sitar and also has an important cello part, played by Jacqueline Thomas. It is all built out of the opening vocal melody that proves to be malleable as the text or the harmony dictates. The chorus, for example ("Though the pages are numbered . . .") states the lines alternating with an instrumental echo. The underlying harmony is often different, so the repetition of the melody does not become monotonous.

The most notable thing about this song is that it includes not just a single modulation, but *three*. The first two (in the body of the song) are of a half-step up (like "I'm So Happy I Can't Stop Crying"), which both have the effect of entering a new "chapter" in the life/book/song; this is the same person, but with a slightly expanded perspective. The last change of key, however, moves down a minor third, for a brief concluding cello solo. It has a kind of deflating effect, perhaps to counteract the overly optimistic sense that the two previous modulations have intimated. Moreover, this final key (of f minor) is actually a half-step *below* our opening key (of f♯ minor). So it does not imply a "return" to where we started from, or even a literal recall. Instead, it may represent the act of remembering one's youth, with a general melancholic air as this song so beautifully captures.

True to the successful pattern of *Ten Summoner's Tales* and *Brand New Day,* Sting closes this album with an upbeat, raucous song.[26] "Sacred Love" is both sexy and spiritual, obvious and deep, and exists, like many of Sting's best songs do, in that exciting space that is both "high" and "low" art. It is a love song that is about the sanctity of sex, and it succeeds in tying together the strands of relationships and spirituality that run through this album.

The biblical references are tightly packed into this song, especially in the fourth verse. "The spirit moves on the water" is a reference to the creation story of Genesis. Passages from the book of John, the crucifixion, Adam and Eve, and the Ten Commandments are all thrown into Sting's songwriting pot to honor the divine spark that is the source of all creation. It is creation, then, that is the purpose of love, and love is the purpose of creation. Sting would also agree, I think, that the word "creation" also encompasses creativity and the producing of music. So it follows that he honors love as sacred, since it is completely woven into the fabric of his career and his life.

A wonderful turn of phrase happens when he refers to two of the Ten Commandments. In verse four, he sings "Thou shalt not covet, thou shalt not steal," and then rhymes that last word with "real." In the next verse he uses the same construction, but with "steal" replacing "covet," and then "kill" as the last word. To rhyme with that: "But if you don't love her your best friend will." This of course addresses the commandment against coveting your neighbor's wife, thus harking back to the previous verse. During the coda, the backing vocals use lines from the first verse (regarding dressing up to make love) as a mantra-like ostinato. Over this Sting lists the connections, for him, between marriage, love, sex, religion, and the Divine Mystery. It is a fitting ending to an overall strong album.

While *Sacred Love* has some excellent tracks that certainly deserve a place next to some of his most popular songs, it is by no means his best work, mainly due to the odd production problem and general lack of melodic ideas. A nice counterpart to the album is the DVD called *Inside: The Songs of Sacred*

Love. It follows the general style of . . . *All This Time* (and has the same director, Jim Gable),[27] in that it shows the band rehearsing the new songs for an upcoming taping session at the Mayan Theater in Los Angeles. This time, however, the interviews and rehearsal footage are interspersed with the concert taping. It was not really a concert, as only a small number of invited guests were in the audience. Sting wanted the songs to be tested in front of an audience, but he didn't want the distraction of a huge cheering crowd.

The DVD is revealing and, for me, gratifying, since I was somewhat disappointed with *Sacred Love*. The new songs work better in this more intimate, less production-heavy environment. The band does not use a traditional drummer, but rather Rhani Krija on percussion and Kipper supplying other necessary electronic beats. "This War" is much more effective on the video, getting a more acoustic-flavored version. And a highlight is the finale of "Whenever I Say Your Name" with Mary J. Blige. The DVD also includes some songs that are not on any album, such as "Like a Beautiful Smile" (which uses Shakespeare's sonnet 18 for most of its text), "All Would Envy" (about a failed marriage between an older man and a young woman), and "That Sinking Feeling" (which is a reworking of "Forget about the Future"). Also included is a treat for classic Police fans: a great stride piano version of "Walking on the Moon" with Jason Rebello.

This documentary seems to capture Sting's very essence: a musician who is constantly challenging himself, always searching for the best way to present a song. That in turn leads to further explorations in the art of songwriting. The live versions of these new songs are already quite different from the "official" renditions on *Sacred Love,* despite the brief period between the recording of the album and the filming of the documentary. On the DVD Sting says: "I've always thought that the album was a kind of starting point . . . something different would happen on stage than in the studio."[28] Sting's ultimate goal is to have a constantly evolving catalogue that can grow and change as he himself does.

Conclusion

This book, like its subject, has come a long way from the punk-tinged white reggae band that suddenly appeared on the international music scene in the late 1970s. If we compare a song like "Sacred Love" to an early track such as "Hole in My Life," there is a world of difference between the two. The earlier song was probably written in a cramped London flat and recorded in the middle of the night at a small studio because the rates were cheaper. The latter song was possibly written in a Tuscan villa and recorded in a state-of-the-art studio that the songwriter owns. Sting has come far. And with over 30 years in the music industry, he shows no signs of slowing down.

At this writing, he is still on the road with The Police, on their enormously successful and well-received reunion tour. The set list featured all of their major hits when I saw them in July 2007 in St. Paul, Minnesota, with some fascinating reworkings of the songs. The band sounded better than ever, if a little grayer. Copeland and Summers were still at the top of their game. Copeland in particular was very impressive in his use of an entire separate "set" of exotic percussion instruments. He used these most visibly on "Walking in Your Footsteps" and "Wrapped around Your Finger."

Sting, as ever, looked and sounded great. He does not seem to have the affliction of many aging rock singers who have a severely compromised upper register. And it appears that the band members have finally made peace. One of the catalysts for the reunion tour was Stewart Copeland's film *Everyone Stares: The Police Inside and Out*. The premiere was in January 2006 at the Sundance Film Festival, and all three band members met after the screening.[1]

The film was almost entirely shot by Copeland, who was constantly seen with a Super 8 camera during The Police years. There is priceless footage of the band's early gigs, all the way up to the "supergroup" years, through the eyes of the drummer. Many of the shots were filmed by mounting the camera behind the drum set, which was a great way to capture the dynamics of the band in performance. There are also several segments of recording sessions at the now-destroyed Air Studios in Montserrat.

In the film, one gets the real sense that Sting is a searcher. He is driven to do the best he possibly can, but there is always something else to seek out, some new knowledge to be gained, a new path to take, a new way to grow. He has certainly grown a great deal since 1978, both as a songwriter and as a person.

An example of this always-searching way of life is the 2006 *Songs from the Labyrinth* recording (and companion DVD, *The Journey & the Labyrinth*). The disc is the culmination of his recent infatuation with a lute that was given to him by Dominic Miller. It is a CD of Renaissance lute songs, mostly by John Dowland (1563–1626), accompanied by Bosnian lutenist Edin Karamazov. The songs are coupled with Sting's own recitation of a letter that Dowland wrote to Sir Robert Cecil, Queen Elizabeth's secretary of state. Dowland, who had converted to Catholicism during the previous reign of Queen Mary, did not get the job as the Protestant Queen Elizabeth's lutenist (a position held by Robert Johnson [ca. 1583–1633]) and so was trying his luck at various courts in continental Europe. The letter was written to try to get into the good graces of the Queen by furnishing Cecil with information on her rivals and enemies.[2] Sting included these excerpts from the letter to give these songs some context and provide a kind of dramatic arc for the CD itself.

The disc was designed to be a "listening experience," with sound design by Kipper that provides ambient sounds such as church bells, rain, and birds. These backgrounds are used under Sting's narration and create seamless transitions between most of the selections. This style of CD production places this disc, whether Sting was aware of it or not, in a recent trend of the Early Music field: that of the "classical concept album," borrowed from the popular music world. Examples of this type of release are *Officium*, by the Hilliard Ensemble with saxophonist Jan Garbarek, and The Dowland Project's thematically centered CDs.

Despite mixed reviews from the classical music world, the album gave Sting yet another No. 1 ranking, this time on the Billboard classical album chart. He freely admits that his is an "unschooled" voice, but many people have noted that English Renaissance singers also lacked formal training, including John Dowland himself. Sting sees a connection between himself and Dowland, whom he calls "the first alienated singer-songwriter."[3]

The 2007 DVD *The Journey & the Labyrinth* goes more in depth about the project, with interviews and video segments shot at Lake House and Il Palagio as well as concert footage of the first performance with Karamazov at St. Luke's Church in London. Once again, Jim Gable directed. And once again, Sting's generosity as a musician and person shines through, as he gives Karamazov a huge amount of credit for realizing this project with him.

In addition to Dowland songs, on the brief tour in 2006–7 the pair performed special arrangements of "Message in a Bottle," "Fields of Gold," and Robert Johnson's "Hellhound on My Trail" (the blues singer, not Queen Elizabeth's lutenist!). With this CD and DVD project, Sting was not just satisfying his personal curiosity about Dowland's music; he also exposed many Sting fans to the world of Renaissance music for the first time, a fact noted by several reviewers,[4] as well as Sting himself: "If I bring a certain percentage of people along from The Police to my own work, and now to a new place, like Dowland, then I feel my job is very satisfying."[5] One is intrigued by what his next undertaking will be, but it would be fruitless to try to second guess someone so creatively curious.

Though Gordon Sumner got his start as a bleached-blond singer and bassist and a member of a genre-defying band that virtually defined New Wave music, his aspiration has always been to be a singer-songwriter. Very early on, his dream was to have people sing his songs, like they do Beatles songs. As he recollected in *Broken Music:*

> I know I want to make my living solely as a musician, but I also want to be recognized as someone unique, defined by my voice, by my abilities as a songwriter, to have the world know my songs and my melodies just as they had known and acknowledged the songs of the Beatles.[6]

In that respect, he has succeeded. A true measure of a song's value is whether it "has legs"; whether other musicians pick it up and make it their own. Sting's catalogue continues to be honored in this way, not only in the frequent use of his songs as film soundtrack material, but also in the number of "covers" that are out there. Everything from the young Canadian "newgrass" band the Duhks doing "Love Is the Seventh Wave," to an all-reggae tribute album to The Police (*Reggatta Mondatta*), to a Corsican band (I Muvrini) singing "Fields of Gold" in their own dialect; all of this creative energy originated from one singer-songwriter's pen. Sting feels that:

> Songs are a little bit like children in a way. You give birth to them . . . and then you watch them grow . . . Other people cover them, adapt them, change them, sample them. And you can only feel pride that your song has now gone into the world and exists as an entity.[7]

One of the points that I hope I have made in this book is that Sting's best songs have a wonderful interplay between music and text. They use melody, harmony, texture, and rhythm to metaphorically illustrate and amplify the meaning of the words. Even if listeners and other musicians are unaware of it, I believe that it is this element of a good songwriter's craft that keeps us coming back to them. With this seamless integration of sound and words, Sting's "children" have grown into old friends.

Selected Discography

Note: Since this book focuses on Sting's work as a composer, I have concentrated on listing songs that he has written. This discography does not include the various performances of other people's songs for soundtracks or concerts. It also focuses on those releases that are truly unique (i.e., singles that have hard-to-find B-sides); some singles with different versions or remixes of the same song have been excluded. All songs listed are by Sting unless otherwise noted. All releases are from A&M unless otherwise noted.

Albums by The Police

Outlandos d'Amour (1978): Next to You, So Lonely, Roxanne, Hole in My Life, Peanuts (Sting/Copeland), Can't Stand Losing You, Truth Hits Everybody, Born in the '50s, Be My Girl/Sally (Sting/Summers), Masoko Tanga.

Reggatta de Blanc (1979): Message in a Bottle, Reggatta de Blanc (Copeland/Summers/Sting), It's Alright for You (Copeland/Sting), Bring on the Night, Deathwish (Copeland/Summers/Sting), Walking on the Moon, On Any Other Day (Copeland), The Bed's Too Big without You, Contact (Copeland), Does Everyone Stare (Copeland), No Time This Time.

Zenyatta Mondatta (1980): Don't Stand So Close to Me, Driven to Tears, When the World Is Running Down You Make the Best of What's Still around, Canary in a Coalmine, Voices Inside My Head, Bombs Away (Copeland), De Do Do Do, De Da Da Da, Behind My Camel (Summers), Man in a Suitcase, Shadows in the Rain, The Other Way of Stopping (Copeland).

Ghost in the Machine (1981): Spirits in the Material World, Every Little Thing She Does Is Magic, Invisible Sun, Hungry for You (J'aurais toujour faim de toi), Demolition Man, Too Much Information, Rehumanize Yourself (Sting/

Copeland), One World (Not Three), Omegaman (Summers), Secret Journey, Darkness (Copeland).

Synchronicity (1983): Synchronicity I, Walking in Your Footsteps, O My God, Mother (Summers), Miss Gradenko (Copeland), Synchronicity II, Every Breath You Take, King of Pain, Wrapped around Your Finger, Tea in the Sahara, Murder by Numbers (Sting/Summers).

SINGLES BY THE POLICE

Fall Out (Copeland)/Nothing Achieving (Copeland). 1977, Illegal.
Roxanne/Peanuts (Sting/Copeland). 1978.
Can't Stand Losing You/Dead End Job (Sting/Copeland/Summers). 1978.
So Lonely/No Time This Time. 1978.
Message in a Bottle/Landlord (Sting/Copeland). 1979.
Walking on the Moon/Visions of the Night. 1979.
The Bed's Too Big without You/Truth Hits Everybody (live). 1980.
Don't Stand So Close To Me/Friends (Summers). 1980.
De Do Do Do, De Da Da Da/A Sermon (Copeland). 1980.
Invisible Sun/Shambelle (Summers). 1981.
Every Little Thing She Does Is Magic/Flexible Strategies (Sting/Copeland/Summers). 1981.
Spirits in the Material World/Low Life. 1981.
Every Breath You Take/Murder by Numbers (Sting/Summers). 1983.
Wrapped around Your Finger/Someone to Talk To (Summers). 1983.
Synchronicity II/Once upon a Daydream (Sting/Summers). 1983.
King of Pain/Tea in the Sahara (live). 1984.
Don't Stand So Close to Me '86/Don't Stand So Close to Me (live). 1986.

COMPILATIONS AND LIVE ALBUMS
BY THE POLICE

Every Breath You Take: The Singles (1986): Roxanne, Can't Stand Losing You, Message in a Bottle, Walking on the Moon, Don't Stand So Close to Me '86, De Do Do Do, De Da Da Da, Every Little Thing She Does Is Magic, Invisible Sun, Spirits in the Material World, Every Breath You Take, King of Pain, Wrapped around Your Finger.

Greatest Hits (1992): Roxanne, Can't Stand Losing You, So Lonely, Message in a Bottle, Walking on the Moon, The Bed's Too Big without You, Don't Stand So Close to Me '86, De Do Do Do, De Da Da Da, Every Little Thing She Does Is Magic, Invisible Sun, Spirits in the Material World, Synchronicity II, Every Breath You Take, King of Pain, Wrapped around Your Finger, Tea in the Sahara.

Message in a Box: The Complete Recordings (1993): Fall Out (Copeland), Nothing Achieving (Copeland), Dead End Job (Sting/Copeland/Summers), Next to You, So Lonely, Roxanne, Hole in My Life, Peanuts (Sting/Copeland), Can't Stand Losing You, Truth Hits Everybody, Born in the '50s, Be My Girl/Sally (Sting/Summers), Masoko Tanga, Landlord (live) (Sting/Copeland), Next to

You (live), Landlord (Sting/Copeland), Message in a Bottle, Reggatta de Blanc (Copeland/Summers/Sting), It's Alright for You (Copeland/Sting), Bring on the Night, Deathwish (Copeland/Summers/Sting), Walking on the Moon, On Any Other Day (Copeland), The Bed's Too Big without You, Contact (Copeland), Does Everyone Stare (Copeland), No Time This Time, Visions of the Night, The Bed's Too Big without You (mono), Truth Hits Everybody (live), Friends (Summers), Don't Stand So Close to Me, Driven to Tears, When the World Is Running Down You Make the Best of What's Still around, Canary in a Coalmine, Voices Inside My Head, Bombs Away (Copeland), De Do Do Do, De Da Da Da, Behind My Camel (Summers), Man in a Suitcase, Shadows in the Rain, The Other Way of Stopping (Copeland), A Sermon (Copeland), Driven to Tears (live), Shambelle (Summers), Spirits in the Material World, Every Little Thing She Does Is Magic, Invisible Sun, Hungry for You (J'aurais toujour faim de toi), Demolition Man, Too Much Information, Rehumanize Yourself (Sting/Copeland), One World (Not Three), Omegaman (Summers), Secret Journey, Darkness (Copeland), Flexible Strategies (Sting/Copeland/Summers), Low Life, How Stupid Mr. Bates (Sting/Summers/Copeland), A Kind of Loving (Sting/Summers/Copeland), Synchronicity I, Walking in Your Footsteps, O My God, Mother (Summers), Miss Gradenko (Copeland), Synchronicity II, Every Breath You Take, King of Pain, Wrapped around Your Finger, Tea in the Sahara, Murder by Numbers (Sting/Summers), Man in a Suitcase (live), Someone to Talk To (Summers), Message in a Bottle (live), I Burn for You, Once Upon a Daydream (Sting/Summers), Tea in the Sahara (live), Don't Stand So Close to Me '86.

The Police Live! (1995) [recorded November 1979]: Next to You, So Lonely, Truth Hits Everybody, Walking on the Moon, Hole in My Life, Fall Out (Copeland), Bring on the Night, Message in a Bottle, The Bed's Too Big without You, Peanuts, Roxanne, Can't Stand Losing You, Landlord (Sting/Copeland), Born in the 50s, Be My Girl/Sally (Sting, Summers). [recorded November 1983]: Synchronicity I, Synchronicity II, Walking in Your Footsteps, O My God, De Do Do Do, De Da Da Da, Wrapped around Your Finger, Tea in the Sahara, Spirits in the Material World, King of Pain, Don't Stand So Close to Me, Every Breath You Take.

Every Breath You Take: The Classics (1995): Roxanne, Can't Stand Losing You, Message in a Bottle, Walking on the Moon, Don't Stand So Close to Me, De Do Do Do, De Da Da Da, Every Little Thing She Does Is Magic, Invisible Sun, Spirits in the Material World, Every Breath You Take, King of Pain, Wrapped around Your Finger, Don't Stand So Close to Me '86, Message in a Bottle (New Classic Rock Mix).

The Very Best of Sting & The Police (2002): Message in a Bottle, Can't Stand Losing You, Englishman in New York, Every Breath You Take, Seven Days, Walking on the Moon, Fields of Gold, Fragile, Every Little Thing She Does Is Magic, De Do Do Do, De Da Da Da, If You Love Somebody Set Them Free, Brand New Day, Desert Rose, If I Ever Lose My Faith in You, When We Dance, Don't Stand So Close to Me, Roxanne, So Lonely.

The Police (2007): Fall Out (Copeland), Can't Stand Losing You, Next to You, Roxanne, Truth Hits Everybody, Hole in My Life, So Lonely, Message in a Bottle, Reggatta de Blanc (Copeland/Summers/Sting), Bring on the Night, Walking on the Moon, The Bed's Too Big without You, Don't Stand So Close to Me, Driven to Tears, Canary in a Coalmine, De Do Do Do, De Da Da Da, Voices Inside My Head, Invisible Sun, Every Little Thing She Does Is Magic, Spirits in the Material World, Demolition Man, Rehumanize Yourself (Sting/Copeland), Every Breath You Take, Synchronicity I, Wrapped around Your Finger, Walking in Your Footsteps, Synchronicity II, King of Pain, Murder by Numbers (Sting/Summers), Tea in the Sahara.

SOUNDTRACK BY THE POLICE

Brimstone & Treacle (original soundtrack, 1982): When the Roll Is Called Up Yonder, Brimstone & Treacle, Narration, How Stupid Mr. Bates (Sting/Summers/Copeland), Only You (Potter/Sting), I Burn for You, Spread a Little Happiness (Ellis/Grey/Newman), We Got the Beat (Caffey) (performed by the Go-Go's), You Know I Had the Strangest Dream, Up the Junction (Difford/Tilbrook) (performed by Squeeze), Bless this House (The Brimstone Chorale), A Kind of Loving (Sting/Summers/Copeland), Brimstone 2.

ALBUMS BY STING

The Dream of the Blue Turtles (1985): If You Love Somebody Set Them Free, Love Is the Seventh Wave, Russians, Children's Crusade, Shadows in the Rain, We Work the Black Seam, Consider Me Gone, The Dream of the Blue Turtles, Moon over Bourbon Street, Fortress around Your Heart.

. . . Nothing Like the Sun (1987): The Lazarus Heart, Be Still My Beating Heart, Englishman in New York, History Will Teach Us Nothing, They Dance Alone (Cueca Solo), Fragile, We'll Be Together, Straight to My Heart, Rock Steady, Sister Moon, Little Wing (Hendrix), The Secret Marriage.

The Soul Cages (1991): Island of Souls, All This Time, Mad about You, Jeremiah Blues (Part I), Why Should I Cry for You? Saint Agnes & the Burning Train, The Wild Wild Sea, The Soul Cages, When the Angels Fall.

Ten Summoner's Tales (1993): If I Ever Lose My Faith In You, Love Is Stronger Than Justice (The Munificent Seven), Fields of Gold, Heavy Cloud No Rain, She's Too Good for Me, Seven Days, Saint Augustine in Hell, It's Probably Me (Sting/Kamen/Clapton), [Everybody Laughed but You (on UK version only)], Shape of My Heart (Sting/D. Miller), Something the Boy Said, Epilogue (Nothing 'Bout Me).

Mercury Falling (1996): The Hounds of Winter, I Hung My Head, Let Your Soul Be Your Pilot, I Was Brought to My Senses, You Still Touch Me, I'm So Happy I Can't Stop Crying, All Four Seasons, [Twenty Five to Midnight (on UK version only)], Valparaiso, Lithium Sunset.

Brand New Day (1999): A Thousand Years (Sting/Kipper), Desert Rose, Big Lie Small World, After the Rain Has Fallen, Perfect Love . . . Gone Wrong, Tomorrow We'll See, Prelude to the End of the Game, [End of the Game (on UK version only)], Fill Her Up, Ghost Story, Brand New Day.

Sacred Love (2003): Inside, Send Your Love, Whenever I Say Your Name, Dead Man's Rope, Never Coming Home, Stolen Car (Take Me Dancing), Forget about the

Future, This War, The Book of My Life, Sacred Love, [some versions include Send Your Love (Dave Aude remix) and/or Shape of My Heart (live)].

Singles by Sting

Spread a Little Happiness (Ellis/Grey/Newman)/Only You (Potter/Sting). 1982.
If You Love Somebody Set Them Free/Another Day. 1985.
Fortress around Your Heart/Shadows in the Rain. 1985.
Love Is the Seventh Wave/Consider Me Gone (live). 1985.
Russians/Gabriel's Message. 1985.
Moon over Bourbon Street/The Ballad of Mack the Knife (Weill/Brecht). 1986.
We'll Be Together/Conversation with a Dog. 1987.
   [From this point forward only CD singles are listed]:
Englishman in New York, Ghost in the Strand, Bring on the Night/When the World Is Running Down (live). 1988.
Fragile, Fragil, Fragilidad, Mariposa Libre (Hendrix). 1988.
They Dance Alone (Cueca Solo), Ellas Danzan Solas (Cueca Sola), Si Estamos Juntos. 1988.
All This Time, I Miss You Kate, King of Pain (live). 1990.
Mad about You, Tempted (live) (Difford/Tilbrook), If You Love Somebody Set Them Free (live). 1991.
The Soul Cages, Walking in Your Footsteps (live), Don't Stand So Close to Me (live). 1991.
It's Probably Me (edit) (Sting/Kamen/Clapton), It's Probably Me (soundtrack version). 1992.
Demolition Man (Soulpower Radio Mix), Demolition Man (film version), King of Pain (live), Shape of My Heart (live). 1993.
Fields of Gold, King of Pain (live), Fragile (live), Purple Haze (live) (Hendrix). 1993.
If I Ever Lose My Faith in You, All This Time (live), Mad about You (live), Every Breath You Take (live). 1993.
Seven Days, January Stars, Mad about You (live), Ain't No Sunshine (live) (Withers). 1993.
Shape of My Heart, The Soul Cages (live), The Wild Wild Sea (live), All This Time (live). 1993.
When We Dance (edit), Fortress around Your Heart (Hugh Padgham remix), When We Dance, If You Love Somebody Set Them Free (Soulpower mix). 1994.
This Cowboy Song (remix featuring Pato Banton), This Cowboy Song (extended remix), When We Dance (classic radio mix), Take Me to the Sunshine. 1995.
I'm So Happy I Can't Stop Crying, This Was Never Meant to Be (Sting/Dudley), Giacomo's Blues, Beneath a Desert Moon. 1996.
I Was Brought to My Senses (Steve Lipson remix), When We Dance, If I Ever Lose My Faith in You, If You Love Somebody Set Them Free. 1996.
Let Your Soul Be Your Pilot (edit), Englishman in New York, The Bed's Too Big without You, Let Your Soul Be Your Pilot. 1996.
You Still Touch Me, Lullaby to an Anxious Child (Sting/Miller), The Pirate's Bride, Twenty Five to Midnight. 1996.

Brand New Day (edit), End of the Game, Windmills of Your Mind (Bergman/ Legrand/Bergman). 1999.

After the Rain Has Fallen (video edit), Seven Days (live), Desert Rose. 2000.

Desert Rose (radio edit), If You Love Somebody Set Them Free (live), Fragile, Desert Rose (CD-ROM video). 2000.

Fragile (new version), Desert Rose (demo version), Fill Her Up (original version), Fragile (video). 2001.

Send Your Love, Moon over Bourbon Street (Cornelius Mix), Send Your Love (Dave Aude remix edit), Send Your Love (video). 2003.

Whenever I Say Your Name, Whenever I Say Your Name (Will.I.Am remix featuring the Black Eyed Peas), Whenever I Say Your Name (Salaam Remi Groove mix). 2003.

Stolen Car (Take Me Dancing) (radio version), Stolen Car (Take Me Dancing) (Batson Doc/Will.I.Am remix), Stolen Car (Take Me Dancing) (B. Recluse mix featuring Twista), Stolen Car (Take Me Dancing) (video). 2004.

MISCELLANEOUS AND SOUNDTRACK
SONGS BY STING

I Can't Say [performed by Ruben Blades on his album *Nothing But the Truth*]. 1988.

All for Love (Adams/Stewart/Sting), [from the film *The Three Musketeers*]. 1993.

Muoio per Te [Italian/English duet version of "Mad about You," performed by Zucchero and Sting on the album *Pavarotti & Friends*]. 1993.

Black and White Army (Bringing the Pride Back Home) [performed by Ryan Molloy]. 1998.

Freak the Mighty [from the film *The Mighty*]. 1998.

Terre D'oru [Corsican/English version of "Fields of Gold," performed by I Muvrini and Sting on the album *Leia*]. 1998.

Until [from the film *Kate & Leopold*]. 2001.

You Will Be My Ain True Love [performed by Allison Krauss and Sting, from the film *Cold Mountain*]. 2003.

Taking the Inside Rail [from the film *Racing Stripes*]. 2005.

COMPILATIONS AND LIVE ALBUMS
BY STING

Bring on the Night (1986): Bring on the Night/When the World Is Running Down, Consider Me Gone, Low Life, We Work the Black Seam, Driven to Tears, The Dream of the Blue Turtles/Demolition Man, One World (Not Three)/Love Is the Seventh Wave, Moon over Bourbon Street, I Burn for You, Another Day, Children's Crusade, Been Down So Long (Lenoir/Atkins), Tea in the Sahara.

... *Nada Como el Sol* (1988): Mariposa Libre (Hendrix), Fragil, Si Estamos Juntos, Ellas Danzan Solas (Cueca Sola), Fragilidad.

Acoustic Live in Newcastle (1991): Mad about You, Ain't No Sunshine (Withers), Island of Souls, The Wild Wild Sea, The Soul Cages.

Fields of Gold: The Best of Sting, 1984–1994 (1994) [International edition]: When We Dance, If You Love Somebody Set Them Free, Fields of Gold, All This Time, Englishman in New York, Mad about You, It's Probably Me (soundtrack version) (Sting, Kamen, Clapton), They Dance Alone (Cueca Solo), If I Ever Lose My Faith in You, Fragile, We'll Be Together (original version), Moon over Bourbon Street, Love Is the Seventh Wave, Russians, Why Should I Cry for You? This Cowboy Song, Fragilidad.

Fields of Gold: The Best of Sting, 1984–1994 (1994) [UK edition]: When We Dance, If You Love Somebody Set Them Free, Fields of Gold, All This Time, Englishman in New York, Mad about You, It's Probably Me (soundtrack version) (Sting, Kamen, Clapton), They Dance Alone (Cueca Solo), If I Ever Lose My Faith in You, Fragile, We'll Be Together (original version), Nothing 'Bout Me, Love Is the Seventh Wave, Russians, Seven Days, Demolition Man (film version).

Fields of Gold: The Best of Sting, 1984–1994 (1994) [U.S. edition]: When We Dance, If You Love Somebody Set Them Free, Fields of Gold, All This Time, Fortress around Your Heart, Be Still My Beating Heart, They Dance Alone (Cueca Solo), If I Ever Lose My Faith in You, Fragile, Why Should I Cry for You? Englishman in New York, We'll Be Together (original version), Russians, This Cowboy Song.

. . . All This Time (2001): Fragile, A Thousand Years, All This Time, The Hounds of Winter, Mad about You, Don't Stand So Close to Me, When We Dance, Dienda (Kirkland/Sting), Roxanne, If You Love Somebody Set Them Free, Brand New Day, Fields of Gold, Moon over Bourbon Street, Shape of My Heart, If I Ever Lose My Faith in You, Every Breath You Take.

The Very Best of Sting & The Police (2002): [same as above].

OTHER RECORDINGS, SOUNDTRACKS, ETC.

Demolition Man (1993) [last five tracks recorded live at Villa Marini, Italy]: Demolition Man (film version), King of Pain, Shape of My Heart, Love Is Stronger Than Justice (The Munificent Seven), It's Probably Me, A Day in the Life (Lennon/McCartney).

The Living Sea (1995) [Some tracks are instrumental arrangements by Steve Wood using several Sting songs]: Fragile, Why Should I Cry for You? (Wood/Sting), Cool Breeze (Wood/Sting), Mad about You (Wood/Sting), Ocean Waltz (Wood/Sting), One World (Not Three)/Love Is the Seventh Wave, Why Should I Cry for You? (Wood/Sting), Saint Agnes & the Burning Train, Tides (Wood/Sting), Why Should I Cry for You? (Wood/Sting), Arrival (Wood), Jellyfish Lake (Wood), Fragile (reprise). Pangaea.

Dolphins (2000) [Some tracks are instrumental arrangements by Steve Wood using several Sting songs. The remaining tracks are from the soundtrack score by Wood.]: I Need You Like This Hole in My Head, Sea of Light (Wood/Sting), Fill Her Up, When Dolphins Dance (Wood/Sting), Ghost Story, First Dive (Wood/Sting), Bubble Rings (Wood/Sting), When We Dance, On the Island (Wood), Dolphins of the World (Wood), Rendezvous (Wood/Sting). Pangaea.

The Emperor's New Groove (2000) [Soundtrack for the Disney film. Sting wrote all the lyrics and collaborated with Dave Hartley on the music. Most of Sting's songs were not used in the film. The remaining tracks are from the soundtrack score by John Debney.]: Perfect World (Sting/Hartley) [performed by Tom

Jones], My Funny Friend and Me (Sting/Hartley), Snuff Out the Light (Yzma's Song) (Sting/Hartley) [performed by Eartha Kitt], Walk the Llama Llama (Sting/Hartley) [performed by Rascal Flatts], Perfect World (reprise), Run Llama Run (Debney), One Day She'll Love Me (Sting/Hartley) [performed by Sting and Shawn Colvin], A New Hope (Debney), Beware the Groove (Debney), The Jungle Rescue (Debney), Pacha's Homecoming/The Blue Plate Special (Debney), The Great Battle/Friends Forever (Debney). Walt Disney Records.

Songs from the Labyrinth (2006) [Featuring Edin Karamazov, lute & archlute. All tracks by John Dowland unless otherwise noted.]: Walsingham, Can She Excuse My Wrongs, Flow My Tears (Lachrimae), Have You Seen the Bright Lily Grow (Robert Johnson), The Battle Galliard, The Lowest Trees Have Tops, Fine Knacks for Ladies, Fantasy, Come, Heavy Sleep, Forlorn Hope Fancy, Come Again, Wilt Thou Unkind Thus Reave Me, Weep You No More, Sad Fountains, My Lord Willoughby's Welcome Home, Clear or Cloudy, In Darkness Let Me Dwell. Deutsche Grammophon.

Filmography

LIVE PERFORMANCES AND DOCUMENTARIES
ON THE POLICE

Police in Montserrat (1981): [see below: bonus material on *Every Breath You Take: The DVD*].

Police around the World (1983): Next to You, Walking on the Moon, Born in the '50s, So Lonely, Man in a Suitcase, Can't Stand Losing You, Bring on the Night, Canary in a Coalmine, Voices Inside My Head, Driven to Tears, When the World Is Running Down You Make the Best of What's Still Around, Shadows in the Rain, De Do Do Do, De Da Da Da, Don't Stand So Close to Me, Roxanne, Truth Hits Everybody, Message in a Bottle.

Outlandos to Synchronicities: A History of The Police Live! (1995): Every Breath You Take, Next to You, Fall Out, Message in a Bottle, Reggatta de Blanc, Can't Stand Losing You, Roxanne, So Lonely, It's Alright for You, The Bed's Too Big without You, Driven to Tears, Walking on the Moon, Demolition Man, Bring on the Night, King of Pain, Wrapped around Your Finger, Every Little Thing She Does Is Magic.

Live Ghost in the Machine (2001, filmed in 1982 at Gateshead Stadium, Newcastle): Message in a Bottle, Every Little Thing She Does is Magic, Walking on the Moon, Spirits in the Material World, Hungry for You (J'aurai toujours faim de toi), When the World Is Running Down You Make the Best of What's Still Around, The Bed's Too Big without You, De Do Do Do, De Da Da Da, Demolition Man, Shadows in the Rain, Driven to Tears, Bring on the Night, One World (Not Three), Invisible Sun, Roxanne, Don't Stand So Close to Me, Can't Stand Losing You, So Lonely.

The Synchronicity Concert (2005, filmed in 1983 at the Omni, Atlanta, Georgia): Synchronicity I, Walking in Your Footsteps, Message in a Bottle, Walking on the Moon,

Wrapped around Your Finger, Hole in My Life, King of Pain, One World (Not Three), Tea in the Sahara, O My God, De Do Do Do, De Da Da Da, Every Breath You Take, Can't Stand Losing You, Spirits in the Material World, So Lonely. DVD bonus tracks: Synchronicity II, Roxanne, Invisible Sun, Don't Stand So Close to Me; also includes an interview before their last show in 1984.

Everyone Stares: The Police Inside Out (2006), directed by Stewart Copeland. A collection of Copeland's own Super 8 footage of The Police's life on the road and in the studio, chosen and edited by him. Begins with the second U.S. tour (spring 1979), and ends at the US Festival in Southern California in September 1982, where they played to their largest crowd ever, approximately 150,000 people. Copeland provided the musical score to the film by "de-arranging" unreleased master tapes.

VIDEO COLLECTIONS OF THE POLICE

Greatest Hits (1992): Roxanne, Can't Stand Losing You, Message in a Bottle, Walking on the Moon, So Lonely, Don't Stand So Close to Me, De Do Do Do, De Da Da Da, Invisible Sun, Spirits in the Material World, Every Breath You Take, Synchronicity II, Don't Stand So Close to Me '86, King of Pain (live), Tea in the Sahara (live).

The Very Best of Sting & The Police (1997): Message in a Bottle, Can't Stand Losing You, Englishman in New York, Every Breath You Take, Seven Days, Walking on the Moon, Fields of Gold, Fragile, Every Little Thing She Does Is Magic, De Do Do Do, De Da Da Da, If You Love Somebody Set Them Free, Let Your Soul Be Your Pilot, Russians, If I Ever Lose My Faith in You, When We Dance, Don't Stand So Close to Me '86, Roxanne.

Every Breath You Take: The DVD (2003, VHS originally released in 1986): Roxanne, Can't Stand Losing You, Message in a Bottle, Walking on the Moon, Don't Stand So Close to Me, So Lonely, De Do Do Do, De Da Da Da, Every Little Thing She Does Is Magic, Invisible Sun, Spirits in the Material World, Every Breath You Take, Wrapped around Your Finger, Synchronicity II, Don't Stand So Close to Me '86. DVD bonus materials: *Police in Montserrat* (BBC documentary filmed in 1981), *Old Grey Whistle Test* TV appearance, 1978 (Can't Stand Losing You, Next to You).

LIVE PERFORMANCES AND DOCUMENTARIES ON STING

Bring on the Night (1985, DVD reissued 2005), directed by Michael Apted. Includes interviews and rehearsal footage with Sting and band members, followed by the concert at Théâtre Mogador, Paris. Rehearsal: Bring on the Night/When the World Is Running Down You Make the Best of What's Still Around, If You Love Somebody Set Them Free, Low Life, Fortress around Your Heart, Love Is the Seventh Wave, Another Day, Shadows in the Rain, Consider Me Gone, Driven to Tears. Concert: Shadows in the Rain, Fortress around Your Heart, We Work the Black Seam, I Burn for You, Children's Crusade, Need Your Love So Bad (Dixon), Roxanne, Russians, Been Down So Long (Lenoir/Atkins), If

You Love Somebody Set Them Free, Demolition Man, Message in a Bottle. DVD bonus videos: Bring on the Night, If You Love Somebody Set Them Free, Russians.

The Soul Cages Concert (1991, The Hague, Netherlands): All This Time, Jeremiah Blues (Part 1), Mad about You, Why Should I Cry for You? Roxanne, Bring on the Night/When the World Is Running Down You Make the Best of What's Still Around, King of Pain, Fortress around Your Heart, The Wild Wild Sea, The Soul Cages, When the Angels Fall, Purple Haze (Hendrix), Walking on the Moon, Message in a Bottle, Fragile.

Sting Unplugged (1991, filmed in New York for MTV): All This Time, Mad about You, Every Breath You Take, Why Should I Cry for You? Message in a Bottle, Tea in the Sahara, Walking on the Moon, The Wild Wild Sea.

Summoner's Travels (1995): If I Ever Lose My Faith in You, Seven Days, Fields of Gold, Straight to My Heart, Synchronicity II, Every Little Thing She Does Is Magic, Englishman in New York, King of Pain, She's Too Good for Me, Nothing 'Bout Me, Every Breath You Take, Fragile.

The Brand New Day Tour: Live from the Universal Ampitheatre (2000, Los Angeles): A Thousand Years, If You Love Somebody Set Them Free, After the Rain Has Fallen, We'll Be Together, Perfect Love . . . Gone Wrong, Seven Days, Fill Her Up, Every Little Thing She Does Is Magic, Ghost Story, Moon over Bourbon Street, Englishman in New York, Brand New Day, Tomorrow We'll See, Desert Rose, Every Breath You Take, Lithium Sunset, Message in a Bottle, Fragile.

. . . All This Time (2001), directed by Jim Gable. Includes interviews with Sting and band members, followed by the concert at Il Palagio: Fragile, A Thousand Years, Perfect Love . . . Gone Wrong, All This Time, Seven Days, The Hounds of Winter, Don't Stand So Close to Me, When We Dance, Dienda, Roxanne, If You Love Somebody Set Them Free, Brand New Day, Fields of Gold, Moon over Bourbon Street, Shape of My Heart, If I Ever Lose My Faith in You, Every Breath You Take. DVD bonus tracks: Every Little Thing She Does Is Magic, Fill Her Up (first section only), Englishman in New York. The documentary contains a complete dress rehearsal performance of Desert Rose with Cheb Mami.

Inside: The Songs of Sacred Love (2003), directed by Jim Gable. Includes interviews with Sting and band members, interspersed with the concert at The Mayan in Los Angeles: Send Your Love, Inside, Dead Man's Rope, Shape of My Heart/ Never Coming Home, Like a Beautiful Smile, Forget about the Future/That Sinking Feeling, This War, Stolen Car (Take Me Dancing)/All Would Envy, Sacred Love, The Book of My Life, Walking on the Moon, Roxanne, Whenever I Say Your Name. Bonus track: Every Breath You Take.

The Journey & the Labyrinth (2007), directed by Jim Gable. Television documentary about the *Songs from the Labyrinth* project. Includes interviews and performances by Sting and Edin Karamazov, as well as behind-the-scenes and live footage. Includes bonus CD of a concert performance with the following tracks: Flow My Tears (Lachrimae), The Lowest Trees Have Tops, Fantasy, Come Again, Have You Seen the Bright Lily Grow (Robert Johnson [ca. 1583–1633]), In Darkness Let Me Dwell, Hell Hound on My Trail (Robert Johnson [1911– 1938]), Message in a Bottle.

VIDEO COLLECTIONS OF STING

Sting: The Videos (1988): If You Love Somebody Set Them Free, Fortress around Your Heart, Love Is the Seventh Wave, Russians, Bring on the Night, We'll Be Together, Be Still My Beating Heart, Englishman in New York, Fragile, They Dance Alone (Cueca Solo).

Ten Summoner's Tales (1993): If I Ever Lose My Faith In You, Love Is Stronger Than Justice (The Munificent Seven), Fields of Gold, Heavy Cloud No Rain, She's Too Good for Me, Seven Days, Saint Augustine in Hell, It's Probably Me (Sting/Kamen/Clapton), Shape of My Heart (Sting/D. Miller), Something the Boy Said, Epilogue (Nothing 'Bout Me).

Fields of Gold, 1984–1994 (1994): When We Dance, If You Love Somebody Set Them Free, Fields of Gold, All This Time, Fortress around Your Heart, Be Still My Beating Heart, Bring on the Night, They Dance Alone (Cueca Solo), If I Ever Lose My Faith in You, Fragile, Why Should I Cry for You? Englishman in New York, Russians, It's Probably Me (Sting/Kamen/Clapton), We'll Be Together, Demolition Man, This Cowboy Song.

The Very Best of Sting & The Police (1997): [same as above].

FILMS FEATURING STING AS AN ACTOR

Quadrophenia (1979), directed by Franc Roddam. Also starring Phil Daniels.

Radio On (1980), directed by Christopher Petit. Also starring David Bearnes.

Artemis 81 (1981), directed by Alastair Reid. Also starring Hywel Bennett, Daniel Day-Lewis.

Brimstone & Treacle (1982), directed by Richard Loncraine, based on the play by Dennis Potter. Also starring Denholm Elliot, Joan Plowright.

Dune (1984), directed by David Lynch, based on the book by Frank Herbert. Also starring Kyle MacLachlan, Jose Ferrer, Max von Sydow.

The Bride (1985), directed by Franc Roddam. Also starring Jennifer Beals.

Plenty (1985), directed by Fred Schepisi, based on the play by David Hare. Also starring Meryl Streep, Sam Neill, Tracy Ullman.

Julia and Julia (Giulia e Giulia) (1987), directed by Peter Del Monte. Also starring Kathleen Turner.

Stormy Monday (1987), directed by Mike Figgis. Also starring Melanie Griffith, Tommy Lee Jones, Sean Bean.

The Adventures of Baron Munchausen (1989), directed by Terry Gilliam. Also starring John Neville, Uma Thurman, Eric Idle.

The Grotesque (also known as either *Gentlemen Don't Eat Poets* or *Grave Indiscretion*) (1995), directed by John-Paul Davidson, based on the novel by Patrick McGrath. Also starring Alan Bates, Theresa Russell, Trudie Styler.

Lock, Stock & Two Smoking Barrels (1998), directed by Guy Ritchie. Also starring Nick Moran, Jason Flemyng, Dexter Fletcher.

Notes

INTRODUCTION

1. Reprinted in *Billboard* 106, no. 22 (May 28, 1994): 5.

2. *The Journey and the Labyrinth* DVD (2007).

3. Craig Zeichner, "Sting Sings Dowland," *Early Music America* 12, no. 3 (Fall 2006): 22.

4. Bill Flanagan, *Written in My Soul: Rock's Great Songwriters Talk about Creating Their Music* (Chicago: Contemporary Books, 1986), 267.

5. Walter Everett, *The Beatles as Musicians: Revolver through the Anthology* and *The Beatles as Musicians: The Quarry Men through Rubber Soul* (New York: Oxford University Press, 1999 and 2001).

6. For a critical and film-theoretical look at Sting's many film roles, see Phil Powrie, "The Sting in the Tale," in *Popular Music and Film,* ed. Ian Inglis (London: Wallflower Press, 2003), 39–60.

7. Sting, *Broken Music: A Memoir* (New York: Dial Press, 2003), 90.

8. Ibid., 99–101.

9. Ibid., 222.

10. Ibid., 259.

11. Ibid., 271.

12. Andy Summers, *One Train Later* (New York: Thomas Dunne Books, 2006), 174.

13. Ibid., 319.

CHAPTER 1

1. Bill Flanagan, "What a Piece of Work Is Sting," *Musician* 154 (August 1991): 42.

2. Andy Summers, *One Train Later* (New York: Thomas Dunne Books, 2006), 176.

3. Quoted in J. D. Considine, "The Police," *Musician, Player and Listener* 38 (December 1981): 60.

4. Albin J. Zak III, *The Poetics of Rock: Cutting Tracks, Making Records* (Berkeley: University of California Press, 2001), 71.

5. All Billboard chart information is from Joel Whitburn's various chart listing publications, listed in the bibliography.

6. Sting, *Lyrics by Sting* (New York: Dial Press, 2007), 47.

7. This was the first song in which Summers used a guitar synthesizer. (Phil Sutcliffe and Hugh Fielder, *The Police: L'Historia Bandido* [London: Proteus Books, 1981], 78.)

8. Walter Everett, *The Beatles as Musicians: Revolver through the Anthology* (New York: Oxford University Press, 1999), 38–39.

9. This couplet is used as a self-referent several times in his later songs and appears in "O My God" and "Seven Days." The meaning of the lines change with each new context and will be discussed in more detail below.

CHAPTER 2

1. Andy Summers, *One Train Later* (New York: Thomas Dunne Books, 2006), 317–19.

2. Art Lange, "Sting and Band: Blue Turtles and Blue Notes," *Down Beat* 52 (December 1985): 18.

3. *Sting.com Discography, Song Details:* "O My God" description, http://www.sting.com/discog/?v=so&a=2&id=207 (Accessed August 26, 2008).

4. Anthony Stevens, *Jung* (Oxford: Oxford University Press, 1994), 42.

5. Ibid., 65.

CHAPTER 3

1. Christopher Sandford, *Sting: Demolition Man* (New York: Carroll & Graf, 1998), 146. See also Andy Summers, *One Train Later* (New York: Thomas Dunne Books, 2006), 4.

2. This show was revived in the 1980s in London. Ellis was president of the Performing Rights Society, which represents Sting in the UK.

3. Sting, *Lyrics by Sting* (New York: Dial Press, 2007), 98.

4. *Los Angeles Times*, June 1985, quoted on www.sting.com: Discography, Release Details, "The Dream of the Blue Turtles," artist comments, http://www.sting.com/discog/?v=a&a=1&id=20 (Accessed August 25, 2008).

5. Vic Garbarini, "Sting under the Gun," *Musician* 82 (August 1985), 31.

6. Ibid., 33.

7. Christian Jahl, *Sting: die Musik eines Rockstars* (Stuttgart: Ibidem-Verlag, 2003), 72.

8. *Record*, June and September 1985, quoted on www.sting.com.

9. Sting can also be heard playing the "cat" theme from this piece during some onstage clowning around in the *Synchronicity* concert DVD (filmed in 1983).

10. Kenneth O. Morgan, *Twentieth-Century Britain: A Very Short Introduction* (Oxford: Oxford University Press, 2000), 6.

11. Vic Garbarini, "Sting's Swing Shift," *Musician* 81 (July 1985), 64.

12. Morgan, *Twentieth-Century Britain*, 87.

13. For a compelling account of how the 1984 strike affected working class families, see the film *Billy Elliot* (2000) directed by Stephen Daldry.

14. The particular synthesizer that Kirkland used here was the Yamaha DX7, a relatively new and ubiquitous instrument at the time (Garbarini, "Sting Under the Gun," *Musician* 82 [August 1985], 32).

15. Sting, Liner notes to *Bring on the Night* CD (1986).

16. "Swing" is a term that generally defines a "jazzy" feel to a rhythm. In most cases, it refers to the way that the quarter note is subdivided: "Swung" eighth-notes place the second eighth a bit later in time than in "straight" eighths. See J. Bradford Robinson, "Swing," *Grove Music Online*, ed. L. Macy, www.oxfordmusiconline.com, (accessed August 31, 2008).

17. I refer the reader to Lawrence Lipton's survey of 1950s jazz and beat culture, *The Holy Barbarians*, in which he characterizes jazz as the "Dyonysian, not the Apollonian, beat in music" (p. 207). I would like to thank Phil Ford for guiding me to Lipton.

18. Although in subsequent writings, Sting has said that the dream actually occurred during the first night of staying and recording in Barbados, well after the decision to go solo and the band's membership had been set (Sting, *Lyrics*, 98).

19. Sting "introduces" interviewer Jools Holland and the camera crew to "Brian," his bass, in the BBC documentary *The Police in Montserrat* (1981, included as bonus material on the DVD reissue of *Every Breath You Take: The DVD* [2003]).

20. Garbarini, "Sting's Swing Shift," 64.

21. Ibid., 65.

22. A typical example of this type of direct, step-up modulation occurs in Jeffrey Osborne's 1982 easy-listening hit "On the Wings of Love." There are countless others.

23. A classic example of this "hidden" modulation occurs in The Beatles' song "And I Love Her." In Sting's catalog, the first time he uses this technique is in "So Lonely," where the guitar solo starts a step up from the previous key and the remainder of the song stays in that higher key. Other Sting songs that have similar harmonic layouts are "Man in a Suitcase," "Low Life," and several songs of his later career.

CHAPTER 4

1. *Timeout*, October 1987, quoted on www.sting.com: Discography, release details, ". . . Nothing Like the Sun," artist comments, http://www.sting.com/discog/?v=a&a=1&id=18 (Accessed August 26, 2008).

2. *Spin*, December 1987, quoted on www.sting.com: Discography, song details, "The Lazarus Heart," artist comments, http://www.sting.com/discog/?v=so&a=1&id=175 (Accessed August 26, 2008).

3. Sting, *Lyrics by Sting* (New York: Dial Press, 2007), 122.

4. *Oxford Dictionary of Quotations*, 2nd ed. (London: Oxford University Press, 1959).

5. Peter Watrous, "How Can You Not Dump on a Guy Like Sting?" *Musician* 110, (December 1987): 64.

6. Sting, Liner notes to . . . *Nothing Like the Sun* (1987).

7. "We Work the Black Seam" also includes a verse in the booklet that was cut from the final version.

8. Peter Manuel, *Popular Musics of the Non-Western World* (New York: Oxford University Press, 1988), 70.

9. Misspelled in the CD booklet as "Gueca."

10. U2, in the song "Mothers of the Disappeared," addressed this same topic on *The Joshua Tree* album a few months before Sting's album was released.

11. The political opposition, being a Marxist-Socialist group, identified strongly with the indigenous people, even if most of the politically active Chileans at this time were not Indians themselves.

12. This point is also made by Christian Jahl, *Sting: die Musik eines Rockstars.* (Stuttgart: Ibidem Verlag, 2003, 86).

13. Blades is one of the pre-eminent band leaders, composers, and voices in salsa. He has also infused salsa with a unique social and political consciousness; previously it was simply thought of as "party music" (Manuel, *Popular Musics,* 48–49).

14. "Fragile" was included on the soundtrack to the IMAX documentary film *The Living Sea* (1995).

15. Phil Sutcliffe and Hugh Fiedler, *The Police: L'historia Bandido* (London and New York: Proteus Books), 36.

16. "Here Comes the Sun," the song that begins side two of The Beatles' *Abbey Road,* is a great example.

17. This is the highest harmony note in the second half of "So Lonely."

18. "Synchronicity I" is in six, and Andy Summers's "Mother" from the same album is in a loping seven.

19. Manuel, *Popular Musics,* 75.

20. The original order of side one of *Sgt. Pepper's Lonely Hearts Club Band,* for example, has a much different effect than the published order: "Sgt. Pepper," "With a Little Help," "A Benefit for Mr. Kite," "Fixing a Hole," "Lucy in the Sky with Diamonds," "Getting Better," and "She's Leaving Home" (CD liner notes by Peter Blake). This is a huge topic in and of itself and is beyond the scope of this book. Suffice it to say that many factors go into choosing the best song sequence, including tempo, mood, key, texture, stylistic genre, song topic, emotional content, and sound quality.

21. Sting, *Broken Music: A Memoir* (New York: Dial Press, 85).

22. "Little Wing" was originally released on the Evans LP *There Comes a Time* (1976). It has since been included on the CD reissues of the Hendrix sessions.

23. The track listing for *The Gil Evans Orchestra Featuring Sting in Perugia* (one of several bootlegs of this concert) is given on Allmusicguide.com as: "Up From the Skies," "Strange Fruit," "Shadows in the Rain," "Little Wing," "There Comes a Time," "Consider Me Gone," "Synchronicity I," "Roxanne," "Tea in the Sahara/ Walking on the Moon," "Instrumental," and "Message in a Bottle."

24. Richard Cook and Brian Morton, *The Penguin Guide to Jazz on CD, LP and Cassette* (London: Penguin, 1992), 356.

25. David Blake, "Hanns Eisler," *Grove Music Online,* edited by Laura Macy, http://www.oxfordmusiconline.com (accessed June 30, 2008).

26. *All This Time* CD-ROM, 1995, quoted on www.sting.com: Discography, song details, "The Secret Marriage," artist comments, http://www.sting.com/discog/?v=so&a=1&id=222 (accessed August 26, 2008).

27. Paintings by Steven Campbell.

28. *Mojo,* February 1995, quoted on www.sting.com: Discography, release details, "The Soul Cages," artist comments, http://www.sting.com/discog/?v=a&a=1&id=17 (accessed August 26, 2008)

29. Sting, *Lyrics,* 144.

30. *St. Paul Pioneer Press,* August 8, 1991, quoted on www.sting.com: Discography, song details, "Island of Souls," artist comments, http://www.sting.com/discog/?v=so&a=1&id=164 (accessed August 26, 2008).

31. Christopher Sandford, *Sting: Back on the Beat* (Boston: Da Capo Press, 2007), 227.

32. Sting, *Lyrics,* 149.

33. See, for example, the song "Changed the Locks" from 1988.

34. Interview on *Timothy White Radio Session,* 1991, quoted on www.sting.com: Discography, song details, "Jeremiah Blues (Part 1)," artist comments, http://www.sting.com/discog/?v=so&a=1&id=171 (accessed August 26, 2008).

35. Kenneth O. Morgan, *Twentieth Century Britain: A Very Short Introduction* (Oxford: Oxford University Press, 2000), 94.

36. Marsalis was not part of *Ten Summoner's Tales* or *Sacred Love* and only played on a few tracks on the remaining two albums.

37. *All This Time* CD-ROM, 1995, quoted on www.sting.com: Discography, song details, "Saint Agnes and the Burning Train," artist comments, http://www.sting.com/discog/?v=so&a=1&id=241 (accessed August 26, 2008).

38. The opening of Yes's "Close to the Edge" has a similar feel, as does some sections of Genesis's "Firth of Fifth."

39. Sting, *Lyrics,* 154.

40. Sting, *Broken Music,* 329.

41. The words "Swim to the light" are printed in the CD booklet just before this recall, which further suggests that the father's soul has been released. This line was apparently cut from the final version of the song and may have helped clarify some of the confusion about what actually happens in the song.

42. Sting, *Lyrics,* 143.

CHAPTER 5

1. Sting, *Lyrics by Sting* (New York: Dial Press, 2007), 161.

2. Ibid., 162.

3. "Old Wardour Castle," *English Heritage* website: http://www.english-heritage.org.uk/server/show/nav.16439.

4. Sting, *Lyrics,* 165.

5. In fact, a good blues song can take any image and give it a sexual connotation; for example, Bessie Smith's recording of "Sugar in My Bones."

6. The chorus does this too, but in c minor.

7. Christopher Sandford, *Sting: Back on the Beat* (Boston: Da Capo Press, 2007), 262.

8. Another possible interpretation is that the narrator is already dead (which would make sense with the title, perhaps), and is reliving why he ended up in hell. It is a bit unclear because there is not a verse explicitly addressing any actual death of the speaker.

9. Prophetically directed at Sting's former accountant Keith Moore, who in 1995 was found guilty of embezzling around $6 million of Sting's money (Sandford 289). Interestingly, Dante also included his real-life enemies among the denizens of the *Inferno*.

10. Sting, *Lyrics*, 177.

11. *Ten Summoner's Tales* promotional interview CD, 1993 (quoted on www. sting.com).

12. Sting, *Lyrics*, 180.

13. Mary K. Greer, *Tarot for Your Self* (N. Hollywood, CA: Newcastle, 1984), 239.

14. Ralph Metzner, foreword to *Choice-Centered Tarot*, by Gail Fairfield (N. Hollywood, CA: Newcastle, 1985), v.

15. The song "Twenty Five to Midnight" (a B-side from the *Mercury Falling* project; not included in the U.S. version) addresses this issue (Sting, *Lyrics* 207). This song will be discussed at the end of this chapter.

16. Espie Estrella, "The AAA Song Form," about.com, Music Education (http:// musiced.about.com/od/othermusicgenres/p/songforms.htm).

17. Sandford, *Sting*, 250.

18. On the British release of this album there are 12 tracks ("Everybody Laughed but You" is not on the U.S. version), and thus the first song, "If I Ever Lose My Faith in You," is listed as the "Prologue." This keeps the number of "tales" to 10.

19. It also ends a song by Beck, "Lonesome Tears," from the album *Sea Change* (2002). This song, however, does not fade but ends inconclusively.

20. *Ten Summoner's Tales* Promotional Interview Disc, 1993 (quoted on www. sting.com).

21. Sandford, *Sting*, 333.

22. *Mercury Falling* Tour Programme, 1996 (quoted on www.sting.com).

23. Sting, *Lyrics*, 192–93.

24. Ibid., 195.

25. Ibid., 195.

26. The dark and brutal quality to the lyric is possibly what drew Johnny Cash to cover this song late in his career, on the album *American IV: The Man Comes Around* (2002).

27. *Q Magazine*, May 1996 (quoted on www.sting.com).

28. Sandford mentions several bad reviews but does not cite them (Sandford, *Sting*, 292–93).

29. However, Sting does not put a lot of significance to this. He writes that the river's name "rhymed nicely with 'mine'" (Sting, *Lyrics*, 198).

30. . . . *All This Time* DVD, 2001.

31. Sting, *Lyrics*, 202.

32. Ibid., 202.

33. Sandford, *Sting*, 219.

34. The reader may recall that the opening bass line is recycled from the coda of "When We Dance."

35. Several possible translations of the French text can be found at Marisa Meister's fan Web site, www.stingetc.com.

36. *US Magazine*, April 1996. The French government conducted a series of nuclear weapons tests in 1995, shortly before the Comprehensive Test Ban Treaty took effect.

37. www.sting.com.

38. Sting, *Lyrics*, 212.

39. Sandford, *Sting*, 293.

CHAPTER 6

1. "Grammy Award Winners: Sting," www.grammy.com (The Recording Academy), http://www.grammy.com/GRAMMY_Awards/Winners/Results.aspx?title=&winner=sting&year=0&genreID=0&hp=1 (accessed August 28, 2008).

2. Sting, *Lyrics by Sting* (New York: Dial Press, 2007), 231. In 2001, Sting returned the favor and sang backing vocals for Mami's hit "Le Rai C'est Chic" (www.sting.com, Discography, release details, "Dellali, Cheb Mami," http://www.sting.com/discog/?v=g&a=1&id=324, accessed August 28, 2008).

3. Sting, *Lyrics*, 231.

4. Ibid., 154.

5. Ibid., 231.

6. Loose translations contributed by fans can be found at www.stingetc.com.

7. Sting, *Lyrics*, 195.

8. Botti has since collaborated with Sting frequently and has gone on to a successful career in the jazz world as a bandleader and soloist.

9. Again, one can find a translation at www.stingetc.com.

10. Sting, *Lyrics*, 242.

11. This version can be heard through www.sting.com.

12. A similar technique was noted in the joyful coda to "They Dance Alone."

13. While not literally based on actual people, Sting has intimated that this song imagines his father Ernie's state of mind after his mother's death (*Music365*, October 1999, quoted on www.sting.com, Discography, song details, "Ghost Story," artist comments, http://www.sting.com/discog/?v=so&a=1&id=143, accessed August 29, 2008).

14. John Miller Chernoff, *African Rhythm and African Sensibility* (Chicago: University of Chicago Press, 1979), 47.

15. Rogier's Police Page, concert archive (http://www.cybercomm.nl/~gugten/tours.htm).

16. Sting, *Lyrics*, 261.

17. Ibid., 266.

18. Interview with Oprah Winfrey on her talk show, aired October 28, 2003. Quoted on www.sting.com: News, Interviews, "The Oprah Show," http://www.sting.com/news/interview.php?uid=1653 (accessed August 29, 2008).

19. Interview with CNN, September 2003 (quoted on www.sting.com: Discography, song details, "Whenever I Say Your Name," artist comments, http://www.sting.com/discog/?v=so&a=1&id=272, accessed August 29, 2008).

20. *BBC Music Magazine*, October 2006 (quoted on www.sting.com: Discography, song details, "Whenever I Say Your Name," artist comments, http://www.sting.com/

discog/?v=so&a=1&id=272). It is possibly Prelude #3 in C# major from Book II of the *Well-Tempered Clavier.* The song does not have exactly the same chord progression, but it is reminiscent of it in spots. It shares a very similar rhythmic profile (a bass note sounded on each beat, followed by an upper part of three sixteenth-notes in an ascending arpeggio pattern).

21. Sting, *Lyrics,* 271. See the introduction to Sting, *Broken Music: A Memoir* (New York: Dial Press, 2003), pp. 1–16 for a riveting account of Sting's first experience taking the drug.

22. See *Broken Music,* 50–51.

23. *Inside: The Songs of Sacred Love,* DVD (2003).

24. Sting, *Lyrics,* 275.

25. Ibid., 281.

26. I am considering this the final song in the sequence, even though various pressings of *Sacred Love* end with other extra tracks.

27. No relation to this author.

28. *Inside: The Songs of Sacred Love,* DVD (2003).

Conclusion

1. Kevin Williamson, "Stewart Copeland Rocks Sundance," *Canoe.ca,* January 21, 2006 (http://jam.canoe.ca/Movies/2006/01/21/1405340.html). Sting actually was at the festival to attend the premiere of Styler's film *A Guide to Recognizing Your Saints.*

2. Sting, Liner notes to *Songs from the Labyrinth.*

3. Ibid.

4. For example, Ann Powers, "Along for the Renaissance Ride," *Los Angeles Times,* January 13, 2007.

5. Quoted in Craig Zeichner, "Sting Sings Dowland," *Early Music America* 12, no. 3: Fall 2006, 20–22.

6. Sting, *Broken Music: A Memoir* (New York: Dial Press, 2003), 226.

7. *Inside: The Songs of Sacred Love* DVD (2003).

Bibliography

Baird, Jock. "Frontman: Sting." *Musician* 174 (April 1993): 7.

Barrow, Steve and Peter Dalton. *The Rough Guide to Reggae*. Third ed. London: Rough Guides, 2004.

The Beatles, Popular Music, and Society: A Thousand Voices, edited by Ian Inglis. New York: St. Martin's Press, 2000.

Benét's Reader's Encyclopedia. Fourth ed., edited by Bruce Murphy. New York: Harper-Collins, 1996.

Berryman, James. *Sting and I: The Totally Hilarious Story of Life as Sting's Best Mate*. London: J. Blake, 2005.

Blake, David. "Hanns Eisler." *Grove Music Online,* edited by Laura Macy. http://www.oxfordmusiconline.com (accessed June 30, 2008).

Blake, Peter. Liner notes to CD reissue of The Beatles' *Sgt. Pepper's Lonely Hearts Club Band*. Capitol Records, 1995.

Borthwick, Stuart and Ron Moy. *Popular Music Genres: An Introduction*. New York: Routledge, 2004.

Brocken, Michael. *The British Folk Revival, 1944–2002*. Aldershot, Hants, England; Burlington, VT: Ashgate, 2003.

Brown, Matthew. " 'Little Wing': A Study in Musical Cognition." In *Understanding Rock: Essays in Musical Analysis,* edited by John Covach and Graeme M. Boone. New York: Oxford University Press, 1997, 155–169.

Chebmami.net. http://www.chebmami.net (accessed June 30, 2008).

Chernoff, John Miller. *African Rhythm and African Sensibility: Aesthetics and Social Action in African Musical Idioms*. Chicago: The University of Chicago Press, 1979.

Clarkson, Wensley. *Sting: the Secret Life of Gordon Sumner*. London: J. Blake, 1996.

Colbert, Paul. "Synchro-city." *Melody Maker* 58, no. 35 (August 27, 1983): 6.

Connelly, Christopher. "Alone at the Top." *Rolling Stone* 416 (March 1, 1984): 17+.

Considine, J. D. "The Police." *Musician, Player and Listener* 38 (December 1981): 58–65.

Cook, Richard and Brian Morton. *The Penguin Guide to Jazz on CD, LP and Cassette.* London: Penguin, 1992.

DeCurtis, Anthony. *In Other Words: Artists Talk About Life and Work.* Milwaukee: Hal Leonard, 2005, 155–162.

Dunn, Jancee. "Q & A: Sting." *Rolling Stone* 779 (February 5, 1998): 26.

Estrella, Espie. "The AAA Song Form," *about.com, Music Education* http://musiced. about.com/od/othermusicgenres/p/songforms.htm (accessed June 30, 2008).

Everett, Walter. *The Beatles as Musicians: Quarry Men through Rubber Soul.* New York: Oxford University Press, 2001.

———. *The Beatles as Musicians: Revolver through the Anthology.* New York: Oxford University Press, 1999.

Flanagan, Bill. "Can We Forgive Sting?" *Esquire* 132, no. 3 (September 1999): 106.

———."Sting Puts the Bass in Its Place: Returning from a Bassman's Holiday." *Musician* 170 (December 1992): 78+.

———. "What a Piece of Work is Sting: the Rock Star Races toward 40." *Musician* 154 (August 1991): 36–40+.

———. *Written in My Soul: Rock's Great Songwriters Talk about Creating Their Music.* Chicago: Contemporary Books, 1986, 259–269.

Fricke, David. "Sting." In *The Rolling Stone Interviews: The 1980s,* by the editors of Rolling Stone. New York: St. Martin's Press/Rolling Stone Press, 1989, 293–299 (originally published in *Rolling Stone* 519 (February 11, 1988): 50–53.

———. "Sting." *Rolling Stone* 512 (November 5–December 10, 1987): 297–298.

Fuller, R. Buckminster. *Critical Path.* New York: St. Martin's Press, 1981.

Furnish, David. "Rock's Bach." *Interview* 26, no. 7 (July 1996): 90+.

Garbarini, Vic. "Sting: At Age 44, Ranting Isn't Enough." *Musician* 217 (December 1996): 11.

———. "Sting's Swing Shift: a Policeman Becomes a Private Eye." *Musician* 81 (July 1985): 56–66.

———. "Sting under the Gun." *Musician* 82 (August 1985): 31+.

Gett, Steve. "Sting: Nothing Like Total Control over Solo Career." *Billboard* 99, no. 49 (December 5, 1987): 19.

Graham, Samuel. "Sting: Rock 'n' roll Intellectual." *High Fidelity* 34, no. 1 (January 1984): 90–92+.

Grammy.com. http://www.grammy.com (accessed June 30, 2008).

Greer, Mary K. *Tarot for Your Self: A Workbook for Personal Transformation.* North Hollywood, CA: Newcastle, 1984.

Henke, James. "Policing the World." *Rolling Stone* 337 (February 19, 1981): 42–48.

Hill, Dave. *Designer Boys and Material Girls: Manufacturing the '80s Pop Dream.* Poole, UK: Blandford Press, 1986, 13–19.

Hirshey, Gerri. "Sting Feels the Burn." *Rolling Stone* 457 (September 26, 1985): 26–28.

Jahl, Christian. *Sting: die Musik eines Rockstars.* Stuttgart: Ibidem Verlag, 2003.

Karpeles, Maud. *An Introduction to English Folk Song.* London: Oxford University Press, 1973.

Lange, Art. "Sting and Band: Blue Turtles and Blue Notes." *Down Beat* 52 (December 1985): 16–18, 51–53.

Lipton, Lawrence. *The Holy Barbarians.* New York: Julian Messner, 1959.

Manuel, Peter. *Popular Musics of the Non-Western World: An Introductory Survey.* New York: Oxford University Press, 1988.

McKenna, Kristine. "A Monster Called Sting." *Rolling Stone* 403 (September 1, 1983): 15–18.

———. "The Police: Making New Wave Safe for America." *Rolling Stone* 310 (February 17, 1980): 13–14.

Meisters, Marisa, ed. *Stingetc.com.* http://www.stingetc.com (accessed June 30, 2008).

Metzner, Ralph. Foreword to *Choice-Centered Tarot,* by Gail Fairfield. North Hollywood, CA: Newcastle, 1985.

Milton, James. *The Police.* New York: Gallery Books, 1984.

Morgan, Kenneth O. *Twentieth-Century Britain: A Very Short Introduction.* Oxford: Oxford University Press, 2000.

Morse, Steve. "Sting-size Music." *St. Paul Pioneer Press,* August 16, 1991.

"Old Wardour Castle." In *English Heritage* Web site: http://www.english-heritage.org.uk/server/show/nav.16439 (accessed June 30, 2008).

The Oxford Dictionary of Quotations. Second ed. London: Oxford University Press, 1959.

Powers, Ann. "Along for the Renaissance Ride." *Los Angeles Times,* January 13, 2007.

Powrie, Phil. "The Sting in the Tale." In *Popular Music and Film,* edited by Ian Inglis. London: Wallflower Press, 2003, 39–60.

Quatrochi, Danny. *Police Confidential.* New York: Beech Tree Books, 1986.

Rice, Anne. *Interview with the Vampire.* New York: Alfred A. Knopf, 1976.

Robertshaw, Nick. "5-inchers Seen as Best Bet among CD Singles in the UK." *Billboard* 99, no. 48 (November 28, 1987): 1.

Rumbold, Judy. "Dedicated to the One I Love: Sting Reflects on Romance, Passion, Trudie Styler—and the Things You Do When You Love Somebody." *Harper's Bazaar* (February 2002), 112+.

Sandford, Christopher. *Sting: Back on the Beat: A Biography.* Boston: Da Capo Press, 2007. Updated version of *Sting: Demolition Man: A Biography.* New York: Carroll & Graf, 1998.

Schruers, Fred. "The Police's Sting Considers a New Career." *Rolling Stone* 364 (March 4, 1982): 47–55.

Shuker, Roy. *Understanding Popular Music.* Second ed. London: Routledge, 2001.

Sischy, Ingrid. "Sting: What Happened When the Bard Questioned the Importance of Music." *Interview* 33, no. 7 (August 2003): 134–5.

Solomon, Jon. "Sting in the Tradition of the Lyric Poet." *Popular Music and Society* 17, no. 3 (1993): 33–41.

Stevens, Anthony. *Jung.* Oxford: Oxford University Press, 1994.

Sting. *Broken Music: A Memoir.* New York: The Dial Press, 2003.

———. *Lyrics by Sting.* New York: The Dial Press, 2007.

———. "The Mystery and Religion of Music." (Berklee College of Music commencement speech, delivered May 15, 1994). Reprinted in *Billboard* 106, no. 22 (May 28, 1994): 5.

Sting.com. http://www.sting.com (accessed June 30, 2008).

Summers, Andy. *One Train Later.* New York: Thomas Dunne Books, 2006.

Sutcliffe, Phil. Liner notes to *Message in a Box: the Complete Police.* A&M Records, 1993.

Sutcliffe, Phil and Hugh Fiedler. *The Police: L'historia Bandido.* London and New York: Proteus Books, 1981.

Van der Gugten, Rogier, ed. *Rogier's Police Page, Concert Archive.* http://www.cybercomm.nl/~gugten/tours.htm (accessed June 30, 2008).

Watrous, Peter. "How Can You Not Dump on a Guy Like Sting?" *Musician* 110 (December 1987): 61+.

Welch, Chris. *The Complete Guide to the Music of The Police & Sting.* London: Omnibus Press, 1996.

Whitburn, Joel. *The Billboard Book of Top 40 Hits.* Eighth ed. New York: Billboard Books, 2004.

———. *Billboard Hot 100 Charts. The Seventies.* Menonomee Falls, WI: Record Research, 1990.

———. *Top Pop Albums, 1955–2001.* Menonomee Falls, WI: Record Research, 2001.

White, Timothy. "Sting's French Sojourn Yields 'Brand New Day.'" *Billboard* 111, no. 38 (September 18, 1999): 1+.

Wild, David. "People of the Year: Sting, Still Platinum after All These Years." *Rolling Stone* 856–857 (December 14–21, 2000): 85.

Williamson, Kevin. "Stewart Copeland Rocks Sundance," *Canoe.ca* (January 21, 2006) http://jam.canoe.ca/Movies/2006/01/21/1405340.html (accessed June 30, 2008).

World Music: The Rough Guide. Vol. 1: Africa, Europe and the Middle East, edited by Simon Broughton, Mark Ellingham, and Richard Trillo. London: The Rough Guides, 1999.

Zak, Albin J. *The Poetics of Rock: Cutting Tracks, Making Records.* Berkeley: University of California Press, 2001.

Zeichner, Craig. "Sting Sings Dowland." *Early Music America* 12, no. 3 (Fall 2006): 20–22.

Index

Middle section: of "Englishman in
New York," 44; of "Forget about
the Future," 104; of "Hole in My
Life," 5; of "Moon over Bourbon
Street," 33; of "Saint Augustine
in Hell," 72; of "She's Too
Good for Me," 71; of "Valparaiso,"
85; of "When We Dance," 77
Miller, Dominic, 62
Miners, 29, 30
"Misterioso" atmosphere, 9, 10, 63
Mixolydian scales, 41, 81
Modulation, 127 n.22; in "The Book
of My Life," 106; in "I'm So
Happy I Can't Stop Crying," 83;
in "Love Is the Seventh Wave," 38;
in "Tomorrow We'll See," 94. *See
also* Hidden modulation; Metric
modulation
Money, 95
Monsters, 17–18
Montserrat, 14
Moon: in "Ghost Story," 96; in "Sister
Moon," 51–52; in "Walking on the
Moon," 7–8; in "The Wild Wild
Sea," 62
"Moon over Bourbon Street,"
32–33
Mothers, 40–41, 42, 51–52
Multi-tracked vocals: in "Bring
on the Night," 37; in "Children's
Crusade," 27; on *Ghost in the
Machine*, 11; in "Hole in My Life,"
5; in "Shape of My Heart," 74
"Murder by Numbers," 15, 19
Muses, 52, 53

Nabokov, Vladimir, 10
"Never Coming Home," 102–3
Noah (Biblical figure), 50–51
Nocturnal mood, 51, 103–4
Northumbrian pipes: in "Fields of
Gold," 69; in "Island of Souls," 55,
57; in "Valparaiso," 85; in "The
Wild Wild Sea," 62
Nostalgia, 69
"Nothing 'Bout Me," 75–76
. . . *Nothing Like the Sun*, 40–41, 47,
51, 54

Nuclear power plants, 29–30
Nuclear war, 19, 24–25, 84–85

Obsession. *See* Love, obsessive
Ocean. *See* Sea
"O My God," 15–16
"One World (Not Three)," 38–39
Outlandos d'Amour, 2, 4

Padgham, Hugh, 11, 14
Pan flute, 46
Patois, 45
Peace, 24
Pedal steel guitar, 85, 94–95
Perfection, 31
"Perfect Love . . . Gone Wrong,"
93–94
Pinochet, Augusto, 46
Pizzicato, 44
Playfulness: in "Brand New Day,"
96–97; in "Epilogue (Nothing
'Bout Me)," 75; in "Forget about
the Future," 105; in "Love Is
the Seventh Wave," 24; in "Love
Is Stronger than Justice (The
Munificent Seven)," 68–69;
on *Ten Summoner's Tales*, 66;
in "Walking on the Moon," 7
Playing cards, 73
The Police: band relations, 14, 19, 20;
break-up of, 19, 20, 30, 35; early
influences, 1; popularity of, 14;
recording sessions of, 11, 14
Police songs, reworked, 27, 37, 78
Poppies, 27
Prayer, 15–16, 101–2
Prokofiev, Sergei, 25–26
Prophecies, 74–75
Prostitution, 2–3, 94
Pub rock, 3
Punk rock, 1–2

Rain: 70, 90, 102
Rainforest Foundation, 30, 54
Rap influences, 38, 44, 93
Rebello, Jason, 103
Reggae, 1–2; in "Demolition Man,"
13; in "History Will Teach Us
Nothing," 45; in "Love Is the

About the Author

CHRISTOPHER GABLE is a freelance composer, musician, and music theory instructor. His music has been performed all across the country, and he has taught at Macalester College and St. Olaf College.